I0438612

Prepared in cooperation with the

Massachusetts Department of Conservation and Recreation, the
Massachusetts Department of Environmental Protection, and the
Massachusetts Department of Fish and Game

Preliminary Assessment of Factors Influencing Riverine Fish Communities in Massachusetts

Open-File Report 2010–1139

U.S. Department of the Interior
U.S. Geological Survey

Preliminary Assessment of Factors Influencing Riverine Fish Communities in Massachusetts

By David S. Armstrong, Todd A. Richards, and Sara L. Brandt

Prepared in cooperation with the
Massachusetts Department of Conservation and Recreation, the
Massachusetts Department of Environmental Protection, and the
Massachusetts Department of Fish and Game

Open-File Report 2010–1139

U.S. Department of the Interior
U.S. Geological Survey

U.S. Department of the Interior
KEN SALAZAR, Secretary

U.S. Geological Survey
Marcia K. McNutt, Director

U.S. Geological Survey, Reston, Virginia: 2010

For more information on the USGS—the Federal source for science about the Earth, its natural and living resources, natural hazards, and the environment, visit http://www.usgs.gov or call 1-888-ASK-USGS

For an overview of USGS information products, including maps, imagery, and publications, visit http://www.usgs.gov/pubprod

To order this and other USGS information products, visit http://store.usgs.gov

Suggested citation:
Armstrong, D.S., Richards, T.A., and Brandt, S.L., 2010, Preliminary assessment of factors influencing riverine fish communities in Massachusetts: U.S. Geological Survey Open-File Report 2010–1139, 43 p.

Acknowledgments

The authors are grateful to the MDCR, MDEP, MDFG, EOEEA, members of the Sustainable Water Management Initiative, and other public agencies, private organizations and individuals for supporting this study. The authors would like to thank M. Freeman (USGS), S. Wenger (Trout Unlimited/U.S. Forest Service), and N. Detenbeck (USEPA) for technical review; and L. Hutchins (MDCR), T. Lamonte and W. Kimball (MDEP), K. Baskin (EOEEA), A. Paul (Alberta FWD), J. Magee (NHFG), and others who provided review comments. Thank you also to L. Ostiguy and P. Steeves (USGS), who provided GIS assistance; the West Trenton Publishing Service Center, who provided editorial review and report layout; and R.Vogel (Tufts University), J. Kennen, J. Coles, B. Cade (USGS), and M. Baker (UMBC) who provided guidance and assistance during the project. The authors would also like to thank the MDFW and MDEP crews who collected the fish samples. The cooperation of public and private landowners who granted permission to access the rivers is appreciated.

THIS PAGE INTENTIONALLY LEFT BLANK

Contents

Figures

Tables

Conversion Factors and other Abbreviations

Inch/Pound to SI

Multiply	By	To obtain
Length		
inch (in.)	2.54	centimeter (cm)
inch (in.)	25.4	millimeter (mm)
foot (ft)	0.3048	meter (m)
mile (mi)	1.609	kilometer (km)
yard (yd)	0.9144	meter (m)
Area		
acre	4,047	square meter (m²)
square mile (mi²)	259.0	hectare (ha)
square mile (mi²)	2.590	square kilometer (km²)
Volume		
gallon (gal)	3.785	liter (L)
gallon (gal)	0.003785	cubic meter (m³)
gallon (gal)	3.785	cubic decimeter (dm³)
million gallons (Mgal)	3,785	cubic meter (m³)
cubic foot (ft³)	0.02832	cubic meter (m³)
Flow rate		
cubic foot per second (ft³/s)	0.02832	cubic meter per second (m³/s)
cubic foot per second per square mile [(ft³/s)/mi²]	0.01093	cubic meter per second per square kilometer [(m³/s)/km²]
gallon per minute (gal/min)	0.06309	liter per second (L/s)
gallon per day (gal/d)	0.003785	cubic meter per day (m³/d)
gallon per day per square mile [(gal/d)/mi²]	0.001461	cubic meter per day per square kilometer [(m³/d)/km²]
million gallons per day (Mgal/d)	0.04381	cubic meter per second (m³/s)
million gallons per day per square mile [(Mgal/d)/mi²]	1,461	cubic meter per day per square kilometer [(m³/d)/km²]

Temperature in degrees Celsius (°C) may be converted to degrees Fahrenheit (°F) as follows:

$$°F=(1.8×°C)+32$$

Temperature in degrees Fahrenheit (°F) may be converted to degrees Celsius (°C) as follows:

$$°C=(°F-32)/1.8$$

Acronyms and Abbreviations

AIC	Akaike's information criterion
DEM	Digital elevation model
EOEEA	Executive Office of Energy and Environmental Affairs
FD	Fluvial dependent
FS	Fluvial specialist
GLM	Generalized linear model
HUC	Habitat Use Classification
IC	Impervious cover
MDCR	Massachusetts Department of Conservation and Recreation
MDEP	Massachusetts Department of Environmental Protection
MDFG	Massachusetts Department of Fish and Game
MDFW	Massachusetts Division of Fisheries and Wildlife
MG	Macrohabitat generalist
NHD	National Hydrography Dataset
NPDES	National Pollutant Discharge Elimination System
OLS	Ordinary least squares
SYE	Sustainable Yield Estimator
TITAN	Threshold Indicator Taxa ANalysis
USGS	U. S. Geological Survey
VIF	Variance inflation factor
WUI	Water-use intensity
YOY	Young-of-the-year
ZINB	Zero-inflated negative binomial

THIS PAGE INTENTIONALLY LEFT BLANK

Preliminary Assessment of Factors Influencing Riverine Fish Communities in Massachusetts

By David S. Armstrong, Todd A. Richards, and Sara L. Brandt

Abstract

The U.S. Geological Survey, in cooperation with the Massachusetts Department of Conservation and Recreation (MDCR), Massachusetts Department of Environmental Protection (MDEP), and the Massachusetts Department of Fish and Game (MDFG), conducted a preliminary investigation of fish communities in small- to medium-sized Massachusetts streams. The objective of this investigation was to determine relations between fish-community characteristics and anthropogenic alteration, including flow alteration and impervious cover, relative to the effect of physical basin and land-cover (environmental) characteristics. Fish data were obtained for 756 fish-sampling sites from the Massachusetts Division of Fisheries and Wildlife fish-community database. A review of the literature was used to select a set of fish metrics responsive to flow alteration. Fish metrics tested include two fish-community metrics (fluvial-fish relative abundance and fluvial-fish species richness), and five indicator species metrics (relative abundance of brook trout, blacknose dace, fallfish, white sucker, and redfin pickerel). Streamflows were simulated for each fish-sampling site using the Sustainable Yield Estimator application (SYE). Daily streamflows and the SYE water-use database were used to determine a set of indicators of flow alteration, including percent alteration of August median flow, water-use intensity, and withdrawal and return-flow fraction. The contributing areas to the fish-sampling sites were delineated and used with a Geographic Information System (GIS) to determine a set of environmental characteristics, including elevation, basin slope, percent sand and gravel, percent wetland, and percent open water, and a set of anthropogenic-alteration variables, including impervious cover and dam density.

Two analytical techniques, quantile regression and generalized linear modeling, were applied to determine the association between fish-response variables and the selected environmental and anthropogenic explanatory variables. Quantile regression indicated that flow alteration and impervious cover were negatively associated with both fluvial-fish relative abundance and fluvial-fish species richness. Three generalized linear models (GLMs) were developed to quantify the response of fish communities to multiple environmental and anthropogenic variables. Flow-alteration variables are statistically significant for the fluvial-fish relative-abundance model.

Impervious cover is statistically significant for the fluvial-fish relative-abundance, fluvial-fish species richness, and brook trout relative-abundance models. The variables in the equations were demonstrated to be significant, and the variability explained by the models, as measured by the correlation between observed and predicted values, ranges from 42 to 65 percent. The GLM models indicated that, keeping all other variables the same, a one-unit (1 percent) increase in the percent depletion or percent surcharging of August median flow would result in a 0.4-percent decrease in the relative abundance (in counts per hour) of fluvial fish and that the relative abundance of fluvial fish was expected to be about 55 percent lower in net-depleted streams than in net-surcharged streams. The GLM models also indicated that a unit increase in impervious cover resulted in a 5.5-percent decrease in the relative abundance of fluvial fish and a 2.5-percent decrease in fluvial-fish species richness.

Introduction

Flow alteration and urban development have been associated with stream ecosystem degradation in flowing waters as measured through fish communities (Karr and Chu, 1999; Freeman and Marcinek, 2006; Zorn, 2008; Poff and others, 2010) and macroinvertebrate communities (Coles and others, 2004; Konrad and others, 2008; Kennen and others, 2009). Streamflow is one of many factors that influence the abundance and distribution of fish, and has been called the master variable because it influences habitat availability, channel geomorphology, and other factors that also influence habitat quality such as water quality and water temperature (Wilding and Poff, 2008; Poff and Zimmerman, 2010). The likelihood that flow alteration and urbanization will degrade aquatic communities is generally acknowledged by the scientific community and by water managers (Poff and Zimmerman, 2010), but the response of aquatic communities to flow alteration relative to the influence of physical basin and land-cover (environmental) characteristics and other anthropogenic factors is poorly understood.

Understanding species-stressor and species-environment relations is an important step toward the conservation of aquatic communities. Several recent studies of fish-community response to flow alteration in southern New England streams have determined that as flow alteration increases, the composition of the fish community shifts as fish dependent upon flow for various stages of their life cycle (fluvial fish) decrease in number (abundance) and richness (number of species) (Armstrong and others, 2001, 2004; Parasiewicz, 2004; Kanno and Vokoun, 2010). Although a decline in fluvial fish metrics is an expected response to increased flow depletion, the level of flow alteration at which responses occur, and the magnitude, rate, and shape of the response curve (for example, linear or nonlinear) are less well understood. Development of quantitative relations among fish-community structure, environmental characteristics, and anthropogenic-alteration variables would benefit water-resource managers in Massachusetts by helping to reduce the uncertainty associated with making management decisions designed to balance human uses with the requirements of fish and wildlife.

Until 2009, streamflow-simulation tools that could be used to estimate streamflows under existing water-use conditions and natural unaltered conditions were unavailable except for basins where streamflow had been simulated by a hydrologic model. However, the U.S. Geological Survey (USGS), in cooperation with the MDEP, recently developed a computer application–the Sustainable Yield Estimator (SYE, version 1.0) (Archfield and others, 2010)–that can be used to estimate altered and unaltered daily streamflows at ungaged sites. The USGS has also developed a series of indicators to characterize flow alteration and other anthropogenic effects for 1,429 subbasins in Massachusetts (Weiskel and others, 2010). These new capabilities, together with new GIS datalayers of percent impervious cover and a comprehensive fish-community database developed by the Massachusetts Division of Fisheries and Wildlife (MDFW), have made possible this statewide assessment of the relations among fish-community response, environmental characteristics, and anthropogenic alteration.

Massachusetts State agencies are interested in determining the effects of flow alterations on fish communities in Massachusetts streams and rivers relative to other measures of anthropogenic alteration, such as impervious surface and dams, and the influence of physical basin characteristics and land-cover characteristics. A 3-year cooperative study was initiated for this purpose in 2009 by the USGS in cooperation with the MDCR. In the fall of 2009, however, Massachusetts State agencies convened the Sustainable Water Management Initiative to begin the process of determining safe-yield values to be used in accordance with the State's Water Management Act to develop a statewide water-allocation program. The Sustainable Water Management Initiative prompted the MDCR, MDEP, and MDFG to fund the USGS to accelerate aspects of the project to help inform development of streamflow criteria. This accelerated investigation necessitated limiting the scope of data collection and data analysis so that a report could be completed within a deadline for safe-yield determinations. After the short-term project has been completed, the USGS plans to continue the investigation using a larger suite of

fish-community and explanatory variables and a wider range of multivariate statistical tools. The results of the accelerated and ongoing studies are expected to provide a scientific basis for the Sustainable Water Management Initiative and will enable water-resource managers to make more informed decisions about managing streamflows and water withdrawals in Massachusetts.

Purpose and Scope

This report describes the results of a preliminary study of the response of stream fish communities in Massachusetts to flow alteration and other measures of anthropogenic stress, such as impervious cover, relative to the effects of environmental characteristics. The report provides bivariate plots among selected fish metrics and measures of flow alteration, impervious cover, and area of open water, with quantile regression curves indicating fish response. The report also presents generalized linear model (GLM) equations and plots that indicate relations between selected fish-response variables and multiple environmental and anthropogenic explanatory variables.

The scope of the study included small to medium streams across Massachusetts but not streams on Cape Cod, the Islands (Martha's Vineyard, Nantucket), and portions of southeastern Massachusetts where information on simulated streamflows was unavailable. Data on fish samples from the MDFW database collected during 1998–2008 were used in the analysis of fish communities; new fish-sampling data were not collected for this study. Analysis focused on riverine fish communities in free-flowing reaches of streams and rivers. Variables analyzed for the study were restricted to a subset of response and explanatory variables selected from a larger set of data collected for the ongoing study. A review of the literature was used to select fish-community variables, measures of anthropogenic stress, and environmental characteristics considered important in determining fish abundance and distribution. Altered and unaltered flows used in the study were simulated for fish-sampling sites using the Sustainable Yield Estimator. The statistical methods employed for analysis were reduced from a larger suite of analytical techniques in order to meet a request by Massachusetts State Agencies for a report on an accelerated timeline.

Description of Study Area

The study sites are on flowing reaches of small- to medium-sized (wadeable) freshwater streams in Massachusetts that were selected from the MDFW database (fig. 1). The MDFW fish-community database contains information on fish-sampling activities conducted in lakes, ponds, streams, and rivers. For the purposes of this analysis, fish-community samples were limited to collections made in free-flowing (non-impounded) reaches of streams because riverine fish are expected to respond to flow alterations in these settings

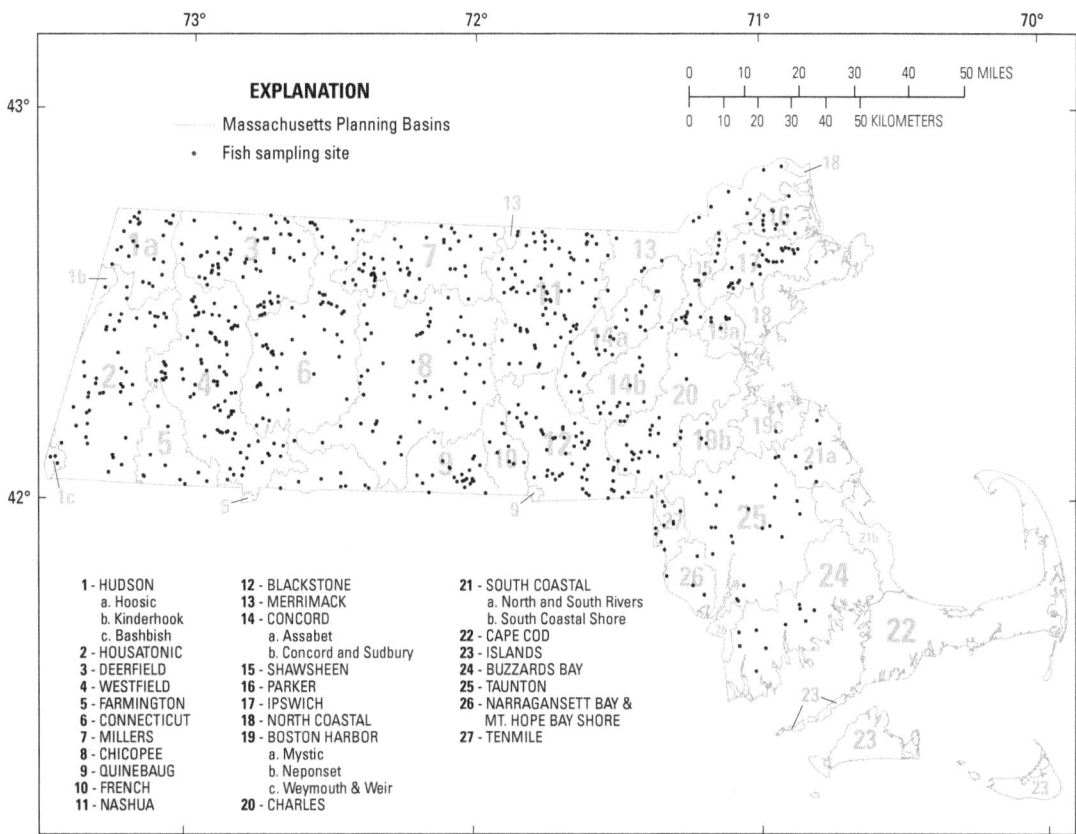

Figure 1. Massachusetts Division of Fisheries and Wildlife fish-sampling sites used to assess environmental and anthropogenic factors influencing fish communities in Massachusetts. Fish samples were collected from 1998–2008.

(Poff and others, 2010; Poff and Zimmerman, 2010). Fish-community samples from lakes, ponds, and reservoirs were not included because fish in these settings were not expected to demonstrate a response to flow alteration. The fish-sampling sites include multiple sites nested within larger drainage basins. The contributing areas to some fish-sampling sites in the study extend into adjacent states. Water use, physical basin characteristics, and land-cover data for the portion of contributing drainage areas outside of Massachusetts are included in the analysis.

The rivers and landscape in Massachusetts have been altered for hundreds of years, to the extent that almost all streams and rivers in the State reflect some aspect of human alteration. Alterations to rivers include physical alterations created by dams, impoundments, road crossings, channelization, and riparian (riverbank) and floodplain development; flow alterations from water withdrawals, diversions, return flows, hydropower, industrial regulation, and urban runoff; and water-quality and sediment alterations caused by wastewater and septic discharges, highway runoff, industrial contaminants, and runoff from urban, suburban, and agricultural land uses. Alterations to rivers are coupled with land-use disturbances that are ubiquitous across the landscape. Land use in Massachusetts is a mosaic of forest, wetland, and open water interspersed with urban, industrial, suburban, and agricultural land, the distribution of which reflects the history of settlement in the region. The distribution of land-use and land-cover characteristics retains close links to geology, topography, river corridors, and transportation routes (Kennen and others, 2009). Even areas classified as mostly forested have some roads, low-density housing, or remnants of historic alterations to the land and waterways. Although large areas of contiguous forest still exist at higher elevations in the Berkshire Mountains in western Massachusetts, many areas in eastern and central Massachusetts are experiencing rapid conversion of forested and agricultural lands to residential and commercial uses (Kennen and others 2009). As a consequence, natural patterns of fish distribution and abundance have been disturbed in many drainage areas in Massachusetts (Hartel and others, 2002).

Previous Studies

The USGS began a series of studies in 1995 to determine the spatial distribution and correlation among characteristics related to aquatic habitats and flow conditions of Massachusetts streams. These studies, done in cooperation with the MDCR, Office of Water Resources (formerly the

Massachusetts Department of Environmental Management), and the MDEP, evaluated several aspects of streamflow requirements and aquatic habitat. Streamflow requirements determined from median daily mean flows for August, and from wetted-perimeter calculations determined from discharge measurements are described by Ries (1997) and Mackey and others (1998), respectively. Relations among stream habitat, fish communities, and hydrologic conditions in the Ipswich River Basin were investigated by Armstrong and others (2001), in the Charles and Assabet River Basins by Parker and others (2004), and in the Sudbury River Basin by Zarriello and others (in press). Streamflows and methods for determining streamflow requirements for aquatic-habitat protection at index stations in southern New England were studied by Armstrong and others (2004) and Parker and others (2004). Armstrong and others (2008) characterized and classified least-altered streamflows in Massachusetts. The effects of flow alteration and increased urbanization on fish and macroinvertebrate communities in southern New England streams are described in Coles and others (2004, 2010), Kennen and others (2009), Meador and others (2008), and Kanno and Vokoun (2010).

Fish species in Massachusetts are described in Hartel and others (2002). Freshwater fish in the southern New England states are characterized by low-species diversity in comparison to the diversity in Midwestern and southeastern United States (Whitworth, 1996; Meador and Carlisle, 2009). Consequently, there are relatively few species in Massachusetts that can be used to detect responses to anthropogenic stressors. The composition of fish communities from relatively unaltered rivers in southern New England and the expected composition of fish communities appropriate for restoration of mainstem rivers (Target Fish Communities) are described in Bain and Meixler (2000; 2008), Parasiewicz (2004), Legros and Parasiewicz (2007), University of New Hampshire and others (2008), and Kashiwagi and Richards (2009).

Factors Limiting Fish Communities

Fish communities are considered to be good indicators of the condition of the habitat in which they live (Karr and Chu, 1999; Poff and Zimmerman, 2010). The distribution and abundance of fish are determined by both environmental and anthropogenic variables at multiple scales (Gido and others, 2006). Many environmental variables play a role in structuring stream fish communities, including flow regime, water quality, stream temperature, habitat availability and connectivity, physical basin characteristics, land cover, and biotic interactions. Anthropogenic changes, such as flow and water-quality alterations, dams and impoundments, and urbanization of land also have large influences on aquatic habitat and fish communities.

Ecological responses to flow alterations include loss of sensitive species, reduced diversity, altered assemblages and dominant taxa, reduced abundance, and increases in non-native species (Poff and Zimmerman, 2010). More than three

decades of research have illustrated the effects of withdrawals and return flows (water quantity), the damming and channelization of streams (physical alteration of stream habitats), and urbanization (physical alteration of the landscape) on aquatic communities including fish (Freeman and Marcinek, 2006; Walsh and others, 2005; Wenger and others, 2009; Poff and Zimmerman, 2010). The result has been a widespread call for streamflows that mimic the magnitude, frequency, duration, timing, and rate of change of natural streamflows (the natural flow regime; Poff and others, 1997, 2010; Richter, 1997; Bunn and Arthington, 2002; Annear and others, 2004). Streamflows in Massachusetts are typically highest in spring and lowest in late summer and early fall. Low flows in summer, which maintain critical habitat that sustains fish communities, including rearing and growth of young fish, correspond with the period of highest human water use and tend to receive the most attention. Flows in other seasons are also important for maintaining stream fish-community integrity. Flood flows in early spring maintain habitat quality by scouring streambeds, modifying channel geomorphology and importing woody debris into stream channels. Moderately high flows in late spring and fall provide opportunities for species to migrate and provide spawning habitat critical for many species. Moderate flows in winter provide stable habitat during harsh winter conditions.

Increased urbanization is associated with declines in aquatic communities (Wang and others, 2001a, 2001b; Meador and others, 2005; Roy and others, 2005; Walsh and others, 2005; Wenger and others, 2008, 2009; Brown and others, 2009b; Cuffney and others, 2010; Baker and King, 2010). These declines are caused by multiple mechanisms, including altered streamflow through increased stormwater runoff and reduced recharge, and altered stream geomorphology through changes in sediment supply, erosion, and filling and piping of headwater channels. Urbanization also degrades water quality by increasing ionic concentrations, nutrients, toxicants, and water temperatures, and by decreasing dissolved oxygen. It degrades fish habitat by removing riparian vegetation, decreasing shade, reducing input of woody debris, and introducing barriers to movement (Wenger and others, 2009). Impervious surface is often used as an indicator of urbanization. Although impervious surface can directly alter streamflow through acceleration of the timing and magnitude of stormwater runoff and alteration of the rates of recharge and evapotranspiration, it is not exclusively a measure of flow alteration but instead represents an accumulation of many factors that together impair the integrity of aquatic communities.

The response of fish to multiple factors confounds the ability to discern the relative importance of individual stressors, such as flow alteration alone (Paul and Meyer, 2001; Brabec and others, 2002; Walsh and others, 2005). For example, poor water quality might limit or reduce the suitability of habitat for fish intolerant to water contamination but might not affect species susceptible to flow alteration, and vice versa. Consequently, it can be difficult to determine which factors or stressors may negatively affect fish habitat at any one place or time or for any given species or fish community.

Methods

Site-specific fish-community information was evaluated in relation to sub-regional and regional-scale environmental characteristics and anthropogenic-alteration variables including impervious cover and streamflow alteration. Information on fisheries was analyzed for 756 stream sampling sites documented in the MDFW fish-community database. Fish metrics were developed for each site using the fish-sampling data collected at the site. Fish metrics analyzed include two fish-community metrics (fluvial-fish relative abundance and fluvial-fish species richness) and five indicator-species metrics (relative abundance of brook trout, blacknose dace, fallfish, white sucker, redfin pickerel). Correlations between flow alterations, impervious cover, and ecological response were determined by use of a space-for-time substitution; that is, ecological conditions are characterized at sites along a gradient of alteration (space) rather than tracking changes in individual species or fish-community composition at a given site as alteration increases over multiple years (time) (Pickett, 1989; Wickham and others, 1997; Carter and others, 2009; Brown and others, 2009a). Two statistical techniques, quantile regression and generalized linear modeling, were applied to determine the association between fish-response variables and the selected environmental characteristics and anthropogenic alteration-explanatory variables.

Streamflow Data and Measures of Flow Alteration

Daily streamflows for altered and unaltered flows were simulated for fish-sampling sites using the Sustainable Yield Estimator (SYE, version 1.0; Archfield and others, 2010). To estimate streamflows at an ungaged site, the SYE first estimates selected streamflow quantiles for an unregulated, daily flow-duration curve by solving regression equations that are a function of physical basin and climate characteristics. A continuous daily flow-duration curve is determined by interpolating streamflow between the estimated quantiles. A time series of unregulated daily streamflow for the 1961–2004 was then created by transferring the timing of the daily streamflow at a selected minimally altered index gage to the ungaged site by equating exceedence probabilities of contemporaneous flow at the two locations. (Archfield and others, 2010). Altered daily streamflows were then estimated using a spatially referenced database of surface-water and groundwater withdrawals and discharges for 2000–2004, using techniques described in Archfield and others (2010) and Weiskel and others (2010). Sampling sites were only included for analysis if they met drainage-area criteria required by the SYE. Thus sites were limited to those having drainage areas greater than 2 mi^2. Streamflows in the mainstems of the Merrimack and Connecticut Rivers were not determined because the SYE application does not provide flow estimates for streamflows in these areas. Streamflows in portions of southeastern Massachusetts, including

Cape Cod and the Islands, were not determined because the SYE application does not provide streamflow estimates for streams in these areas unless the groundwater contributing areas to the fish-sampling sites are delineated, which was not done for this preliminary study.

Flow alteration often involves simultaneous modification of several components of the flow regime in combination with the effects of altered land use. Flow alterations that are accounted for in the SYE water-use database include surface-water and groundwater withdrawals for municipal and non-municipal water supply, wastewater returns from sewage-treatment plants, and return flows from point sources permitted by the MDEP and the National Pollutant Discharge Elimination System (NPDES) and from septic systems. Surface-water withdrawals from reservoirs are included only in annual flow-alteration statistics. Details on the withdrawal and discharge data used by the SYE to determine altered flows have been reported previously in the Massachusetts Water Indicators report (Weiskel and others, 2010). Streamflows simulated by SYE do not directly include non-consumptive flow alterations caused by industry, hydroelectric facilities, manipulation of water-level releases by reservoirs, or alterations to flow regimes caused by altered land use or impervious surfaces. However, some of these flow alterations may be present to varying degrees in the streamflow records of the index gages used by SYE to determine the timing of daily flows.

The SYE produces screening-level estimates of daily streamflows by applying current (2000–2004) monthly median water use estimates to over 40 years of simulated unaltered streamflow conditions (1960–2004). Comprehensive water use data for 1960–2004 are not available. Consequently, although annual and monthly variations of flows are well represented, daily streamflow values likely differ from those actually experienced by fish sampled in the streams.

Streamflow statistics used as indicators of streamflow alteration in this study were selected from those used by Weiskel and others (2010). These statistics include percent alteration of August median flow, percent alteration of annual flow, and water-use intensity (WUI). The percent alteration flow statistics were calculated as 1 minus the ratio of altered flow to unaltered flow, multiplied by 100. Percent alteration of August median flow was selected because in Massachusetts it represents the seasonal period of lowest flows, highest temperatures, and highest human water demand. The signs for the percent alteration of August median flow and percent alteration of annual-flow statistics represent depleted and surcharged flows; a negative percent alteration represents a depletion, and a positive percent alteration represents a surcharge. The percent alteration of August median flow was highly correlated with percent alteration of other low-flow months, precluding their use together in the same analyses. The WUI indicator is a ratio defined as the sum of the absolute value of withdrawals and return flows relative to the long-term average unaltered streamflow from a basin (Weiskel and others, 2007; 2010). The WUI indicator is used to identify "churned" basins, where human flows (withdrawals and return flows) are similar in magnitude to each other, yet large relative to unaltered streamflows from the basin. Four additional indicators were tested as explanatory variables: the ratio of annual return flows to annual unaltered flows (return-flow fraction), the ratio of withdrawals to unaltered flows (withdrawal fraction), and mean annual and August median flows normalized to cubic feet per second per square mile.

Fish-Community Data and Fish Metrics

Fish samples used in this analysis were limited to those in the MDFW database. The fish samples were collected during the summer base-flow season (typically mid-June to mid-September) using MDFW protocols designed to gather a cross section of the fish community in wadeable streams (Appendix 1 of Armstrong and others, 2008). The fish-community data in the MDFW fish database were collected, with few exceptions, by the MDFW for statewide monitoring purposes and not specifically to address the potential effects of flow alteration or impervious surface on fish-community structure.

The MDFW fish database required screening to select the fish sample data used in this study. Fish samples were limited to those collected by use of backpack and barge electrofishing gear (pulsed direct current) during a single upstream pass. Single-pass backpack electrofishing has been determined to be an effective and reliable approach for obtaining community-wide estimates (species richness) (Price and Peterson, 2010). Data were screened for efficiency, method parity, and interdependence. Efficiency screening was done to improve sample consistency and fish-capture efficiency, and to exclude sites where sampling conditions precluded capture of a representative cross section of the fish community. Sites were removed for reasons including high water, turbid water, and equipment failure. Stream reaches were evaluated for sample length and length-to-width ratio. Stream reaches of greater than 91 meters (100 yards) were included. Reaches less than 91 meters were scrutinized for length-to-width ratio to ensure that the habitat was sufficiently sampled. Samples as short as 30 meters were included only if the average stream width was 1 meter or less. Samples with multiple-pass-removal methods were corrected to reflect the sampling effort conducted at single-pass sites. Any fish captured in passes other than the first pass were removed, and the data were corrected to include only the shocking time from the first pass.

Fish metrics were developed for each site by use of fish-sampling data collected at each sample site. Fish samples from multiple sites were not combined for use in this study. The MDFW database included many sites that were sampled multiple times over nearly a decade. To reduce pseudoreplication (samples that are not independent) and spatial autocorrelation of environmental variables (similarity among variables based on the proximity of sample sites), sites used in this study were restricted to those that were greater than 0.5 km from each other (Wenger and others, 2008). Sites that were closer than 0.5 km were identified as a family of sites. The sample from each family with the largest watershed area was included in this study. In the event of a tie, a site was selected randomly. Family identification was retained as a variable in the dataset with the intent of examining temporal variability at a later date.

Only year-round-resident freshwater fish species were included in the fish analysis (table1). The occurrence of non-resident individuals can be unpredictable and not representative of site-specific environmental conditions (Angermeier and Karr, 1986). Anadromous fish (alewife, blueback herring, American shad, striped bass, sea lamprey) and estuarine fish (mummichogs) were excluded. These species are uncommon in the MDFW samples and all life stages are not in the river systems for the entire sampling period. American eel, a catadromous species, was included in the analysis, as the species enters freshwater when juvenile and spends the majority of its adult life (potentially 15 years) in freshwater systems. Trout greater than 200 mm were excluded to avoid including trout stocked as adults in the analysis. All Atlantic salmon were excluded as these fish were stocked as fry as part of the Atlantic salmon restoration effort. Landlocked salmon were not removed, however, as they are produced from natural reproduction. Fish smaller than 40 mm, representing early life stage young-of-the-year (YOY), were excluded because of difficulties in sampling, identification, patchy distribution, and exceedingly high year-to-year variability in production that can occur from natural causes (such as a period of lower than average air temperatures or exceedingly high or low flows) or by anthropogenic disturbances. Removal of YOY is a recommended practice in the development of Indexes of Biotic Integrity (IBIs) (Halliwell and others, 1999; Angermeier and Karr, 1986) because their numbers can be highly variable through the summer season and because they can occur in large numbers seasonally, potentially skewing a dataset (Angermeir and Karr, 1986). To exclude YOY fish, all fish less than 40 mm were removed.

Fish-community response variables selected for testing in the study included metrics determined from habitat-use classifications and temperature classifications. These classifications were determined to be those most likely to indicate a range of response and have been acknowledged to provide insight into anthropogenic alteration in terms of both water quantity and quality.

Fish were assigned a habitat-use classification on the basis of published life-history traits (Bain and Meixler, 2000, 2008; Halliwell and others, 1999; Kashiwagi and Richards, 2009). The classification includes fluvial specialists (FS), fluvial dependents (FD), and macrohabitat generalists (MG) (table 1). Fluvial specialists, such as blacknose dace and fallfish, require flowing-water habitats throughout their life cycle (Bain and Meixler, 2008). Fluvial dependents, such as common shiners and white sucker, require access to streams or flowing-water habitats for a specific life stage but otherwise can be found in lakes, reservoirs, and rivers. Macrohabitat generalists, such as pumpkinseed and redfin pickerel, use a

Table 1. Common and scientific names of fishes, species codes, and habitat use classifications for each species.

[Kashiwagi and Richards (2009) Species Code: Massachusetts Division of Fisheries and Wildlife species abbreviaton. HUC (Habitat Use Classification): FD, fluvial ; FS, fluvial specialist; MG, macrohabitat generalist; -- species not categorized.]

Common name	Species Code	Scientific name (Genus and species)	HUC
Petromyzontidae (lampreys)			
American brook lamprey	BL	*Lampetra appendix*	--
Anguillidae (freshwater eels)			
American eel	AE	*Anguilla rostrata*	MG
Cyprinidae (carp and minnows)			
Goldfish	G	*Carassius auratus*	MG
Lake chub	LC	*Couesius plumbeus*	MG
Common carp	C	*Cyprinus carpio*	MG
Cutlips minnow	CLM	*Exoglossum maxillingua*	FS
Common shiner	CS	*Luxillus cornutus*	FD
Golden shiner	GS	*Notemigonus crysoleucas*	MG
Bridle shiner	BM	*Notropis bifrenatus*	MG
Spottail shiner	SS	*Notropis hudsonius*	MG
Bluntnose minnow	BNM	*Pimephales notatus*	MG
Blacknose dace	BND	*Rhinichthys atratulus*	FS
Longnose dace	LND	*Rhinicthys cataractae*	FS
Creek chub	CRC	*Semotilus atromaculatus*	FS
Fallfish	F	*Semotilus corporalis*	FS
Catostomidae (suckers)			
Longnose sucker	LNS	*Catostomus catostomus*	FD
White sucker	WS	*Catostomus commersoni*	FD
Creek chubsucker	CCS	*Erimyzon oblongus*	FS
Ictaluridae (bullhead catfishes)			
White catfish	WC	*Ameiurus catus*	MG
Yellow bullhead	YB	*Ameiurus natalis*	MG
Brown bullhead	BB	*Ameiurus nebulosus*	MG
Tadpole madtom	TMT	*Noturus gyrinus*	FS
Esocidae (pike and pickerels)			
Redfin pickerel	RP	*Esox americanus americanus*	MG
Northern pike	NP	*Esox lucius*	MG
Chain pickerel	CP	*Esox niger*	MG
Umbridae (mudminnows)			
Central mudminnow	CM	*Umbra limi*	--
Salmonidae (salmon, chars, and trout)			
Rainbow trout	RT	*Oncorhynchus mykiss*	FS
Landlocked salmon	LLS	*Salmo salar*	FD
Brown trout	BT	*Salmo trutta*	FS
Brook trout	EBT	*Salvelinus fontinalis*	FS
Fundulidae (killifishes)			
Banded killifish	K	*Fundulus diaphanus*	MG
Cottidae (sculpins)			
Slimy sculpin	SC	*Cottus cognatus*	FS

Table 1.   Common and scientific names of fishes, species codes, and habitat use classifications for each species.—Continued

[Kashiwagi and Richards (2009) Species Code: Massachusetts Division of Fisheries and Wildlife species abbreviaton. HUC (Habitat Use Classification): FD, fluvial ; FS, fluvial specialist; MG, macrohabitat generalist; -- species not categorized.]

Common name	Species Code	Scientific name (Genus and species)	HUC
Moronidae (striped basses)			
White perch	WP	*Morone americana*	MG
Centrarchidae (sunfishes and black basses)			
Rock bass	RB	*Ambloplites rupestris*	MG
Banded sunfish	BS	*Enneacanthus obesus*	MG
Redbreast sunfish	RBS	*Lepomis auritus*	MG
Green sunfish	GSF	*Lepomis cyanellus*	MG
Pumpkinseed	P	*Lepomis gibbosus*	MG
Bluegill	B	*Lepomis macrochirus*	MG
Smallmouth bass	SMB	*Micropterus dolomieu*	MG
Largemouth bass	LMB	*Micropterus salmoides*	MG
Black crappie	BC	*Pomoxis nigromaculatus*	MG
Percidae (perches and darters)			
Swamp darter	SD	*Etheostoma fusiforme*	MG
Tesselated darter	TD	*Etheostoma olmstedi*	FS
Yellow perch	YP	*Perca flavescens*	MG

broad range of habitat; they include species commonly found in lakes, reservoirs, and rivers and can complete their life cycle in any one of these systems. For the purposes of this preliminary report, the fluvial-specialist and fluvial-dependent species were combined into a single fluvial classification.

Fish metrics were developed on the basis of counts of the various taxa and were expressed in terms of fish relative-abundance (in counts per hour of electrofishing), proportional-abundance, and species richness. The relative-abundance, proportional abundance, and species richness metrics each represent different aspects of a fish community. For example, the fluvial-fish relative-abundance metric reflects the overall abundance of fluvial fish, regardless of species, and is a useful metric for Massachusetts because not all fluvial-fish species are distributed statewide. The fluvial-fish species-richness metric is a measure of the diversity of fluvial-fish species, but does not reflect the abundance of individual species. The fluvial fish proportional abundance metric is a measure of the fluvial composition of the fish community relative to species classified as macrohabitat generalists.

A set of relative-abundance metrics were determined for five indicator species (brook trout, blacknose dace, fall-fish, white sucker, and redfin pickerel). These species were selected to represent a range of sensitivities to anthropogenic stress (pollution tolerant and intolerant species), mesohabitat preference (fluvial and generalist species), and temperature tolerances. The species also represent a range of biological attributes (maximum body size, migration habits, and

home-range sizes) which together provide information on fish species statewide.

Environmental Characteristics

The environmental factors selected for testing as explanatory variables in this study were primarily sub-regional to regional-scale physical basin characteristics and natural land-cover characteristics. These environmental characteristics are not expected to change substantially over short-term periods unless altered by anthropogenic activities. Land-use variables, such as the developed, high-, medium-, and low-intensity landcover classes determined from the National Land-Cover Database (NLCD) (U.S. Geological Survey, 2000), were not included in this preliminary report. Environmental variables used in the study were selected because they had been indicated in the literature to be related to fish-community attributes. Contributing drainage basins to the fish-sampling sites were delineated from a 10-meter digital elevation model (DEM) in ESRI ArcGIS using an automated batch procedure from Arc Hydro Tools. Stream networks were obtained from the high-resolution National Hydrography Dataset (NHD) (U.S. Geological Survey, 1999b). Environmental characteristics were determined for the contributing areas to the fish-sampling sites using a Geographic Information System (GIS) and were compiled from a variety of GIS data sources and clearinghouses (table 2 in Armstrong and others, 2008). GIS layers used were all projected in a NAD 83 State Plane Massachusetts Mainland, FIPS zone 2001 GIS projection.

Landscape-scale factors are known to structure fish assemblages through their association with finer-scale habitat features and variables that can have a physiological effect on organisms (Creque and others, 2005; Gido and others, 2006; Austin, 2007). Environmental characteristics used in this study include contributing drainage area, elevation, basin slope, channel gradient, percent area of sand and gravel, and percent area of wetland and open water. Some of the land-cover characteristics, such as percent area of open water, are also influenced by human activities (most lakes and ponds in Massachusetts are augmented by or formed entirely by dams) and are discussed as both environmental characteristics and anthropogenic alterations in this report.

The contributing drainage area to a site can be used as an indicator of stream size. Fish-species composition in large- and medium-sized rivers differs from that in small streams and brooks; larger streams are expected to include a more diverse fish community (Goldstein and Meader, 2004). Fish-species richness also tends to vary with elevation; fish communities at higher elevations typically contain fewer species than those at lower elevations (Wickham and others, 1997). Stream gradient generally covaries with velocity and substrate, and these variables can influence fish-community composition; some fish species or life stages prefer high-gradient stream habitats but others occupy low-gradient reaches (Argent and others, 2003). High-gradient streams typically have a higher prevalence of gravel, cobble, boulder, or rock substrate, whereas sand and silt substrates and aquatic vegetation are more common in low-gradient streams. In the glaciated Northeast, a high percent area of sand and gravel in a basin generally indicates aquifers that discharge groundwater to streams (Randall, 2001). Streamflow during prolonged dry periods between storms (base flow) is maintained primarily by groundwater discharge to streams; and streams that have a higher percent area of sand and gravel generally have higher base flows (Ries, 1999). Ground-water discharge also contributes to cool summer water temperatures that are critical for supporting coldwater fish communities. Large areas of wetland and open water in a drainage basin can moderate the variability of streamflow and alter water temperature and quality. Large areas of open water, which include areas of impoundments as well as that of lakes and ponds, also provide increased habitat for spawning and recruitment of macrohabitat generalist species into stream systems.

Physical basin characteristics and land-cover characteristics at the basin scale are not expected to explain large amounts of the variation in fish communities. Basin-scale characteristics likely explain the variation in fish communities only to the extent that the basin-scale characteristics are correlated to finer-scale habitat features and physical conditions that are directly relevant to fish, such as stream velocity, water quality, water temperature, and habitat space available for different life stages, or other important factors, such as environmental stability and ecosystem productivity (Poff

and others, 1997; Cereghino and others, 2005). Local habitat data (such as stream width, substrate, stream velocity, water depth) and mesohabitat information (riffle, run, pool) were not available for analysis. Consequently, local channel slope, which often covaries with these features, was estimated using GIS for each fish-sampling site. To calculate channel slope, elevations were first determined along the centerlines using the LongestFlowPath tool in Arc Hydro (ESRI) and then extracted by intersecting a 300-meter buffered circle, centered at the fish-sampling site, with the stream centerline. Channel slope was then calculated for the reach upstream from the fish sampling point by first determining the difference in elevation between the elevation of the upstream point on the centerline at the intersection of the 300-meter circle and the elevation of the downstream sampling point, and then dividing by the length of the centerline between these points.

The location of each fish-sampling site (Outlet X, Outlet Y) was also included in the analysis. Outlet X and Outlet Y were calculated as the X and Y coordinates (in meters) divided by 10,000, respectively. Coordinates were determined from a NAD 83 State Plane Massachusetts Mainland FIPS zone 2001 GIS projection. Outlet X and Outlet Y increase in value from west to east, and south to north, respectively. Location variables co-vary with a number of variables that vary across Massachusetts, including climate, topography, geology, and land use. Because some anthropogenic stresses also follow an east-west gradient (for example, impervious cover), it is difficult to determine whether some species are present or absent as a result of post-glacial distribution or as a result of localized extirpations caused by past or current land and water use.

Indicators of land-cover alteration in the contributing areas were summarized by use of 1-meter resolution impervious-cover (IC) data (Massachusetts Office of Geographic and Environmental Information, 2007). The impervious-cover data for contributing basin areas outside of Massachusetts were determined using methods described in Weiskel and others (2010). Dam locations were obtained from a database maintained by the MDFG Division of Ecological Restoration Program. The presence of dams and impoundments in a basin were indicated primarily by measures of dam density per square mile and dam density per stream mile, and secondarily by area of open water. Open-water area includes areas of impoundments, natural lakes, and natural lakes augmented by dams.

Land use in a narrow corridor extending upstream throughout an entire stream network has been shown to be an effective predictor of fish communities (Van Sickle and Johnson, 2008). Consequently, the percent area of impervious cover within a 240-m buffer adjacent to the stream (BFIC) was also included as a variable in the study. A 240-m buffer width (120-m outward in both directions from the stream centerline) was used to be consistent with values published in Coles and others (2004).

Statistical Analysis

Two analytical techniques, quantile regression and generalized linear modeling, were applied to determine the association between fish-response variables and environmental characteristics and anthropogenic-alteration explanatory variables. Both quantile regression and generalized linear modeling are linear modeling techniques. Nonlinear models were not tested for this preliminary report.

Quantile Regression

The ecological concept of limiting factors indicates that species will be abundant if no other factors are limiting, but if one or more factors are limiting, the species will be constrained to lower abundance than expected (Cade and others, 2005). For example, even if flow alterations are nonexistent or minimal, fish habitat may be poor for some species if other requirements such as water-quality conditions conducive to fish survival are not met. Bivariate scatter plots of species and stressor variables illustrate the concept of limiting factors when data display a right-skewed, wedge-shaped relation distributed below an upper bound. The declining upper bound indicates that the explanatory variable can act as a constraint on the given response variable and also illustrates the maximum abundance of a species given ideal environmental conditions. The wedge shape of scatter plots indicates that the relations between the plotted variables exhibit high variability. This high variability arises when other environmental or biologic variables function as active limiting factors and keep the response variable from reaching the upper constraint line (Thomson and others, 1996; Cade and Noon, 2003; Schooley and Wiens, 2005; Anderson, 2008).

A correlation analysis of a dataset that displays a wedge-shaped relation may be an insufficient tool for identifying relations between variables. Likewise, measures of central tendency such as lines indicating mean and median values, may not represent the response of all portions of the data. For example, a high density of points near the origin can make a correlation coefficient positive even though the upper edge of the data has a negative slope.

Quantile regression is valuable for illustrating the upper limits of fish-response variables in relation to a stressor gradient and for indicating the direction of that association. Quantile regression can be used to estimate functional relations between variables for all portions of a probability distribution (Cade and Noon, 2003; Koenker, 2005), but it is used in this report only to estimate rates of change for functions along or near the upper boundary of the conditional distribution of responses. Viewing variables as constraints rather than as correlates can show that changes near the maximum response better represent effects when the measured factor is the limiting constraint (Cade and others, 2005). Regression quantiles near the upper boundary of a wedge-shaped relation describe potential rather than actual patterns of a species relative abundance and distribution (Vaz and others, 2008).

Quantile regression fits a regression line such that a defined proportion of the data points fall above the line and the remainder of the points fall below the line (Cade and Noon, 2003). For example, for the 0.90 quantile (90th quantile), 90 percent of the observations are below the fitted regression line. The 90th quantile has been used as a robust quantile to describe the upper bounds of wedge-shaped relations (Scharf and others, 1998; Wang and others, 2001a, 2001b) and was selected over larger quantiles, such as the 95th quantile, to ensure sufficient points were used to estimate of the slope of the regression line (Konrad and others, 2008).

Quantile regression models for this study were fit in the software program R (R Development Core Team, 2008), using the rq package of Koenker (2005). The rq package fits a linear model. Nonlinear quantile regression functions also can be estimated but were not tested for this preliminary report. Estimates of linear quantile regression were determined for the logs of the response variable (y). A small constant was added before determining the logarithms because there were some zero counts. These linear quantile regressions were returned to a nonlinear form by back-transformation (exponentiating). A back-transformation was possible because regression quantiles retain their statistical properties under any monotonic transformation of y (Cade and Noon, 2003; Cade and Guo, 2000; Koenker and Machado, 1999). That is, the 90th quantile of the transformed data is equivalent to the 90th quantile of the original data. The resulting regression line plots as a curve on a scatter plot of the data, the shape of which is appropriate for modeling relations with a wedge-shaped form (Wang and others, 2001a).

A bootstrap procedure, by which the dataset is resampled with replacement within the range of observed and predicted values, was used to obtain standard errors and confidence intervals. Confidence intervals can indicate that the ecological response is relatively imprecise if confidence intervals are wide and can indicate reliability if the 95-percent confidence interval excludes zero. Quantile regression models are insensitive to extreme values of response variables and can deal with zero counts, which are common in species-distribution models of abundance data (Cade and others, 1999; Vaz and others, 2008).

Quantile regression is a univariate technique useful for determining the association between two variables (Creque and others, 2005). However, multiple environmental and anthropogenic factors interact to influence the local abundance and distribution of fish. If additional uncontrolled factors are measured and analyzed in a multivariable analysis (such as with a GLM model), some of the multiple factors that interact to produce the wedge-shaped scatter plots can be revealed.

Generalized Linear Models and Extensions

Ordinary Least Squares (OLS) multiple linear regression is commonly used to model multivariable relations in a dataset but is not appropriate for the dataset used for this study. OLS multiple linear regression requires the response variable to be normally distributed and model residuals to be normally distributed with a constant variance across all values of the explanatory variables. Scatter plots of many of the fish-response variables and anthropogenic-alteration variables tested in this study exhibit a wedge shape, violating the variance homogeneity assumption. Although it is common for fish-community data to have non-normal distributions that are highly skewed, many of the fish-response variables also contain a high number of zero values. Response variables that are highly skewed with many zero observations cannot be made normal by any transformation. Finally, fish-community metrics are typically expressed in units such as abundance (counts), ratios (percent), or presence-absence (binary) for which linear regression may not be appropriate. Rather than force data to fit linear regression models, generalized linear models (GLMs) and their extensions are increasingly used to develop regression equations for data with these characteristics (Zuur and others, 2007, 2009; Bolker, 2008; Wenger and Freeman, 2008).

A GLM extends linear models in two ways: it allows the response variable to have a distribution other than normal, and it allows for a transformation of the response variable (Ahmadi-Nedushan and others, 2006). A GLM enables models to be developed for response variables that are bounded (as in proportions), cannot be negative (as in counts) or have highly skewed distributions, and allows a more flexible variance structure in the fitted model. These characteristics allow GLMs to be applied to a wider range of data than traditional linear models, and to include linear regression models as a special case.

A GLM has many analogies to an OLS multiple linear regression model in that it predicts or models a response variable (dependent variable) from one or more explanatory variables (independent variables), and the right side of the GLM equation remains a linear function of explanatory variables. A GLM differs from an OLS multiple linear regression model, however, because the assumption that the relation between the explanatory variables and the response variable is linear is not incorporated into a GLM. A GLM specifies a nonlinear link function that equates the linear combination of explanatory variables with a function of the response variable (McCullagh and Nelder, 1989). This is similar to a data transformation of the response variable in OLS regression. Selection of the link function is dictated by the nature of the response variable. GLMs can accommodate response variables from the exponential distribution family. For example, a log link is used for count data that have a Poisson distribution, and a logit link is used for response variables that are proportions and have a binomial distribution. Once the model is fitted, the predicted values of the response variable (the mean value of Y) are obtained by applying the inverse of the link function (for example, exponentiating if a log link is used).

GLMs also differ from OLS multiple linear regression by using maximum likelihood techniques to determine GLM equation coefficients and minimizing residuals of the fitted model rather than minimizing the sums-of-squares

(McCullagh and Nelder, 1989). Consequently, although there are tools available for GLMs that can be used for model selection, and summary statistics such as parameter estimates, standard errors, and goodness-of-fit statistics that can be used to evaluate fitted GLMs, these tools are different than the familiar statistics used for this purpose in OLS models, such as the coefficient of determination (R^2) and variance-inflation factors (VIF).

A GLM with a negative binomial distribution can be used to model count data such as species abundance or richness. By definition, the negative binomial distribution consists of positive integers with a mean (μ) and a variance ($\mu + [\mu/k]$). The parameter k is called a dispersion parameter and allows the variance to be larger than the mean. Negative binomial distributions with small values of k are positively skewed with a high number of observations equal to zero. The probability of observing a value $y = 0, 1, 2...n$ in a variable that has a negative binomial distribution is given by equation 1 (Zuur and others, 2009):

$$Pr_{NB}(y) = \frac{\Gamma(y + 1/k)}{\Gamma(y+1)\Gamma(1/k)} \frac{(\mu k)^y}{(1 + \mu k)^{y + 1/k}} \quad (1)$$

where

$Pr_{NB}(y)$	=	probability of observing y from a negative binomial distribution,
μ	=	mean of negative binomial distribution,
k	=	dispersion parameter, and
$\Gamma(y)$	=	gamma function: $(y\text{-}1)!$

When y is a rate, μ is replaced by $a\mu$, where μ is the count and a is the unit time. Models for rates such as catch per unit effort are fit with an offset to account for differing sampling times.

A high number of excess zeros, as observed in this fish-sampling dataset, can lead to a characteristic that is called overdispersion. Overdispersion occurs when there is greater variability in a dataset than would be expected on the basis of the probability distribution assumptions of the statistical model. Although a negative binomial distribution can accommodate very skewed datasets, the presence of a large number of zeros can cause a negative binomial model to be overdispersed. This overdispersion violates the statistical assumptions of many analytical methods that are commonly used to predict species-environment relations and may lead to increased uncertainty regarding parameter estimates, cause the p-values of model coefficient estimates to be unreliable, and lead to poor model selection (Lewin and others, 2010). When the number of zeros is so large that the data do not fit standard distributions (for example, normal, Poisson, negative binomial), the dataset is referred to as "zero inflated" (Martin and others, 2005; Brainwood and others, 2008).

Analysis of zero-inflated data requires application of techniques that are flexible concerning the distributional properties of the data. Zero-inflated negative binomial (ZINB) models are an extension of GLMs designed to accommodate discrete datasets that are overdispersed as a result of excessive zeros. Multivariable ZINB models are used in ecological studies to model species abundance and richness (Arab and others, 2008; Wenger and Freeman, 2008; Martin and others, 2005; Zuur and others, 2009). ZINB models consider two types of zeros in the data. Structural zeros occur when a species is absent from a site owing to unsuitable habitat or habitat degradation and represent real ecological effects on a population. They may also be a result of a species that does not saturate its entire suitable habitat or has a low frequency of occurrence (rare species). Sampling zeros refer to zeros that occur when a species was present but undetected, or when a site was suitable for a species but the species was not present at the time of sampling owing to other, unknown stochastic processes (Cunningham and Lindenmayer, 2005; Martin and others, 2005).

ZINB models use a mixture distribution to account for sampling zeros separately from structural zeros and non-zero observations. The models are composed of two terms. The first term determines the probability of a sample containing zero counts, and the second term governs the magnitude of the count. Because the count portion of the model determines the probability for cases where positive catches may occur, but are not certain, the count term also determines a portion of the zero values. Sampling zeros follow a Bernoulli distribution (that is, they can take a value of only 0 or 1) and are modeled by a logistic regression where π is the probability of a sampling zero. Nonzero counts and structural zeros are modeled by a negative binomial regression and have a detection probability of $(1-\pi)$. The probability of observing $y = 0, 1, 2...n$ for the mixed distribution is given by equation 2 (Zuur and others, 2009),

$$Pr_{ZINB}(y) = \begin{cases} \pi + (1 - \pi)\, Pr_{NB}(y) \ \ for \ y = 0 \\ (1 - \pi)\, Pr_{NB}(y) \ \ for \ y > 0 \end{cases} \quad (2)$$

where

$Pr_{ZINB}(y)$	=	probability of observing y from the mixed distribution,
π	=	probability of zero from the Bernoulli process, and
$Pr_{NB}(y)$	=	probability of observing y from the negative binomial process.

For a particular set of covariates, the zero-inflated negative binomial equation is

$$E(Y) = \mu(1 - \pi) \quad (3)$$

where

$E(Y)$	=	expected mean value of relative abundance or species richness and where
π	=	probability of a zero from the logistic portion of the equation, calculated as

$$\pi = \frac{e^{\gamma_0 + \gamma_1 z_1 + \gamma_2 z_2 + \cdots + \gamma_i z_i}}{1 + e^{\gamma_0 + \gamma_1 z_1 + \gamma_2 z_2 + \cdots \gamma_i z_i}}$$

and where

μ	=	mean value of relative abundance or species richness from the negative binomial count portion of the equation, calculated as

$$\mu = e^{\beta_0 + \beta_1 x_1 + \beta_2 x_2 + \cdots + \beta_j x_j}$$

and where

γ_i	=	coefficient of logistic component,
β_j	=	coefficient of negative binomial component,
z_i	=	covariates for the logistic model, and
x_j	=	covariates for the negative binomial model.

Only one outcome $E(Y)$ is predicted by the ZINB model. However, some insight into factors determining the distribution and abundance of response variables can be gained by examining the different explanatory variables or covariates that are determined for the logistic and count parts of the model. The ZINB mixture models differentiate between explanatory variables that predict the absence of a species, and explanatory variables that primarily predict the abundance of a species for sites where the species occur (Wenger and Freeman, 2008). For example, for a species with a limited geographic range, presence/absence of a species may be predicted by the logistic portion of the model by use of geographic location as a covariate, whereas, in areas where the species is likely to occur geographically, abundance may be predicted by the count portion of the model by covariates that describe habitat suitability.

Model Fitting and Validation

ZINB models were fit in the R statistical software program (R Core Development Team, 2008) using the pscl package (Zeileis and others, 2008). Stepwise model selection was performed from a pool of potential explanatory variables including physical basin characteristics, land cover, percent impervious cover, and water-use indicators. Several criteria were used to compare models. Log likelihood ratio tests were used to compare the selected regression model to the null model containing only the intercept. Akaike's information criterion (AIC) (Akaike, 1974) was used to compare nested models. The AIC employs the log likelihood to measure the lack of a model fit relative to the number of explanatory variables in the model; as the number of variables in the model increases, the lack of fit decreases, and the penalty for having too many variables increases (Burnham and Anderson, 2002; Kennen and others, 2009). Models with a lower AIC have a better fit.

Vuong's test (Vuong, 1989) was used to compare the goodness of fit between non-nested models.

There is no widely accepted measure of predictive power for GLMs, such as the coefficient of determineation (R^2) used for OLS regression. AIC and likelihood ratio tests are measures of relative goodness-of-fit between two nested models and are appropriate for selecting between potential fitted models, but they do not indicate the predictive ability or amount of variance explained by a particular model. The predictive ability of a GLM is often examined by comparing observed and model-predicted values. Because of the distributional properties of a ZINB model, the correlation coefficient between predicted and observed values cannot be used to calculate the R^2 of a model, such as in OLS linear regression; however, it does give a relative indication of the amount of variation in the data explained by the model (Zheng and Agresti, 2000). Alternatively, a simple linear regression between the observed and predicted values provides information about the bias of the fitted GLM (Potts and Elith, 2006; Sileshi and others, 2009). For a simple linear model of the form: $Observed_i = \beta_0 + \beta_1 Fitted_i$, an intercept of 0 and a slope of 1 for the simple linear regression indicates an unbiased GLM fit. An intercept significantly different from zero indicates a prediction bias, and a slope significantly different from one indicates an inconsistent bias across the range of predictions. Taken together, the coefficients of a linear model for predicted versus observed, along with the correlation coefficient, give a complete picture of the goodness-of-fit and predictive ability of a GLM.

Relations Among Flow Alteration, Impervious Cover, and Fish Communities

The following sections describe streamflow alteration, fish-community composition, and environmental characteristics for the 756 fish-sampling sites. Results are summarized from the application of two analytical techniques, quantile regression and generalized linear modeling, to evaluate the association between fish-response variables and selected environmental characteristics and anthropogenic-alteration explanatory variables. Results are not shown for all explanatory variables tested during the study. Relations between some of the indicator species and stressor gradients were determined to be nonlinear and were not appropriate for application of the quantile regression models fit for this preliminary report; likewise, GLM models for some fish-response metrics were not significantly different than the null model or indicated extreme bias, and so are not shown. These issues are discussed further in the various sections.

Data Exploration

The following sections discuss the streamflow alteration, fish-community characteristics, and environmental characteristics represented by the 756 fish-sampling sites used in this study.

Streamflow Alteration

The estimated (altered) August median flows for the study sites, normalized by drainage area, ranged from 0.0 to 1.6 ft³/s/mi², with a median value of 0.21 ft³/s/mi². Mean annual flows, normalized by drainage area, ranged from 0.53 to 2.7 ft³/s/mi², with a median value of 2.0 ft³/s/mi².

The degree and range of percent alteration of August median flow represented by the 756 fish-sampling sites used in this study were compared to those reported in Weiskel and others (2010) for 1,429 subbasins and groundwater contributing areas in Massachusetts (fig. 2). The comparison indicated a similar range of percent flow alteration and distribution shape; however, the fish-sampling sites were weighted slightly more toward less-altered conditions for flow-depleted sites and toward slightly more-altered conditions for flow-surcharged sites. The percent alteration of August median flows at the fish-sampling sites ranged from 100 percent depleted to 373 percent surcharged. Most sites exhibited only a small amount of flow alteration. The interquartile range (which includes the middle 50 percent of the data) ranged from -0.03 to 0.02 percent alteration of August median flow.

Of 756 fish-sampling sites used in the analysis, 67 percent were in net-depleted streams and 33 percent were in net-surcharged streams, under median August conditions. Thirteen

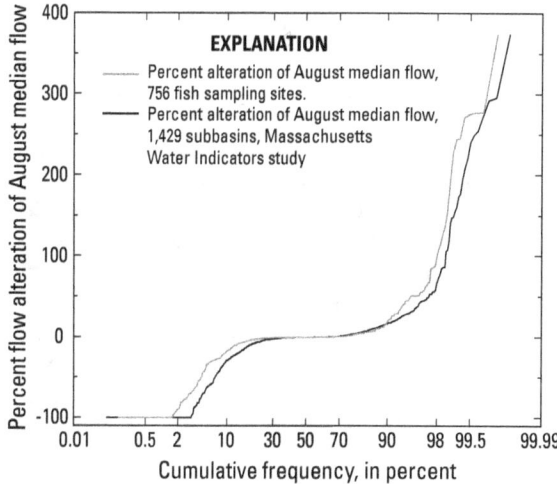

Figure 2. Cumulative frequency in relation to percent alteration of August median flow for 756 Massachusetts Division of Fisheries and Wildlife fish-sampling sites and 1,429 subbasins and groundwater contributing areas across Massachusetts (Weiskel and others, 2010).

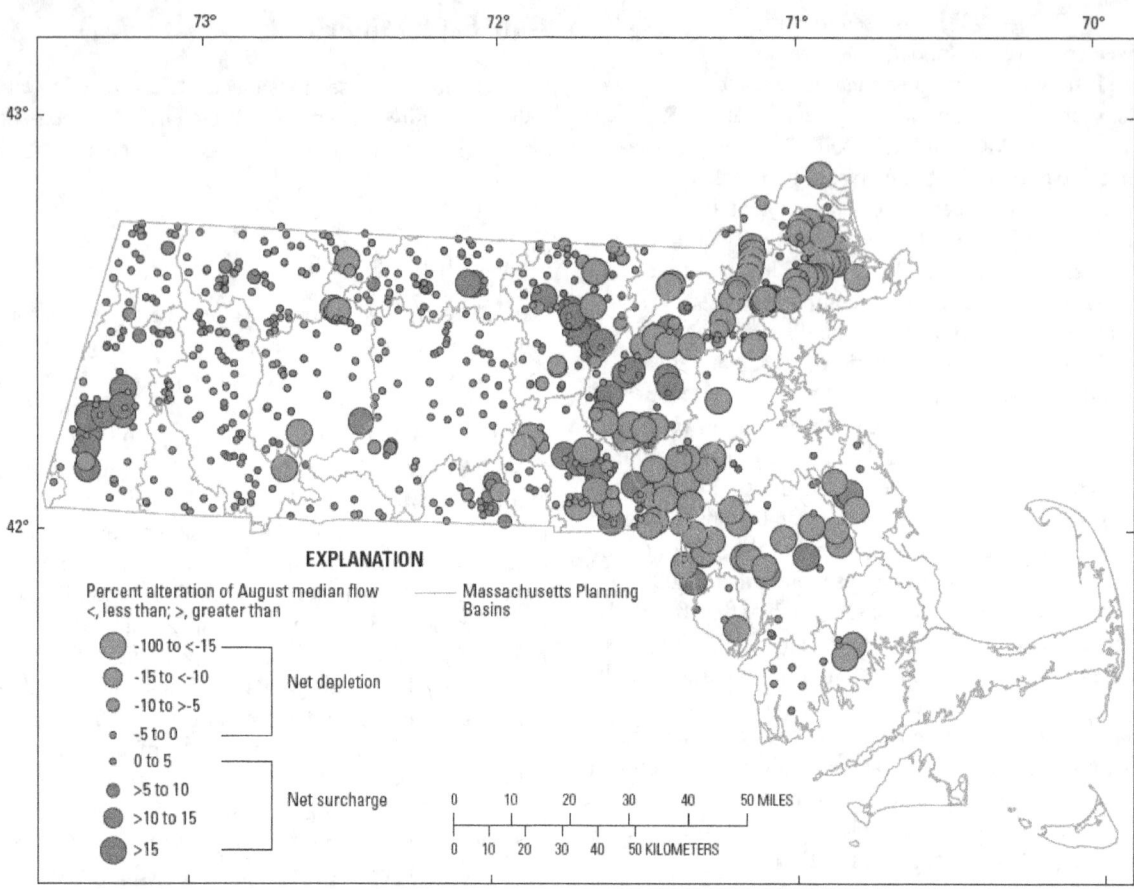

Figure 3. Percent alteration of August median flows at 756 Massachusetts Division of Fisheries and Wildlife fish-sampling sites, 1998–2008.

percent of the sites were indicated to have greater than 10-percent depletion under median August conditions, and twelve percent of the sites had greater than 10-percent surcharging under these conditions. A map of the percent alteration of August median flow for the fish-sampling sites used for this study (fig. 3) indicates that the majority of sites that have a net surcharge or net depletion of greater than 10-percent alteration of August median flows are in the highly populated areas just outside of the Massachusetts Water Resources Authority (MWRA) Boston-MetroWest water and sewer service area.

The WUI indicator ranged from 0 percent to 282 percent of unaffected flows. Under long-term average conditions, 74 percent of the fish-sampling sites were indicated to have water-use intensities of less than 5 percent, and only 8 percent of the fish-sampling sites had greater than 20 percent WUI, whereas statewide values were 64 percent and 12 percent, respectively (Weiskel and others, 2010).

Fish-Community Data

The fish-community data analyzed included 92,222 individual fish of 45 species from 756 fish-sampling sites. However, only 23 of these species occurred at greater than 5 percent of the sites. The five most common species in terms of species occurrence among sites were white sucker, blacknose dace, brook trout, pumpkinseed, and longnose dace (table 2A). These five species were each present at about 52, 49, 42, 37, and 35 percent of the sites, respectively. The maximum observed species richness at a site was 15, (range 0–15), and the mean and median values for the observed species richness were 6 species. In terms of total abundance, 20 species accounted for greater than 95 percent of the total number of fish sampled. The five most common species in terms of abundance were blacknose dace, white sucker, longnose dace, brook trout, and fallfish (table 2B). Fish relative abundance, measured as the number of fish sampled per hour of electrofishing, ranged from 0 to 2,500.

Fish-species and fish-community metrics were assessed graphically for outliers, and underlying assumptions were assessed for statistical tests. As expected, histograms of the

Table 2. Common names of fish, and number and percentage of sites sorted by the number of sites at which each species was captured, and number and percentage of individuals sorted by the number of individuals captured at sites used for the preliminary assessment of fish communities in Massachusetts.

Common name	Number of sites	Percent of sites	Common name	Number of individuals	Percent of individuals
White sucker	389	51.87	Blacknose dace	25,254	27.38
Blacknose dace	369	49.20	White sucker	8,086	8.77
Brook trout	318	42.40	Longnose dace	8,015	8.69
Pumpkinseed	277	36.93	Brook trout	7,316	7.93
Longnose dace	260	34.67	Fallfish	5,532	6.00
Bluegill	220	29.37	Slimy sculpin	5,466	5.93
Fallfish	194	25.87	Common shiner	5,132	5.56
Largemouth bass	186	24.80	Redfin pickerel	3,424	3.71
Chain pickerel	183	24.40	American eel	2,948	3.20
American eel	180	24.00	Pumpkinseed	2,733	2.96
Yellow bullhead	177	23.60	Bluegill	2,417	2.62
Redfin pickerel	175	23.33	Creek chub	1,940	2.10
Common shiner	172	22.93	Brown trout	1,818	1.97
Tesselated darter	154	20.53	Tesselated darter	1,815	1.97
Brown trout	135	18.00	Yellow bullhead	1,007	1.09
Brown bullhead	134	17.87	Largemouth bass	979	1.06
Slimy sculpin	134	17.87	Redbreast sunfish	972	1.05
Golden shiner	130	17.33	Rock bass	967	1.05
Yellow perch	114	15.20	Golden shiner	889	0.96
Creek chub	108	14.40	Yellow perch	841	0.91
Redbreast sunfish	56	7.47	Smallmouth bass	745	0.81
Banded sunfish	54	7.20	Chain pickerel	714	0.77
Creek chubsucker	45	6.00	Spottail shiner	658	0.71
Smallmouth bass	37	4.93	Bluntnose minnow	561	0.61
Rock bass	35	4.67	Brown bullhead	481	0.52
Swamp darter	30	4.00	Banded sunfish	381	0.41
Longnose sucker	25	3.33	Landlocked salmon	258	0.28
Spottail shiner	19	2.53	Longnose Sucker	237	0.26
Bluntnose minnow	13	1.73	Creek chubsucker	156	0.17
Black crappie	12	1.60	American brook lamprey	79	0.09
Green sunfish	11	1.47	Swamp darter	63	0.07
Landlocked salmon	9	1.20	Lake chub	63	0.07
Lake chub	8	1.07	Rainbow trout	46	0.05
Rainbow trout	8	1.07	Common carp	46	0.05
American brook lamprey	6	0.80	Cutlips minnow	40	0.04
Banded killifish	5	0.67	Green sunfish	32	0.03
Bridle shiner	4	0.53	Central mudminnow	26	0.03
Common carp	3	0.40	Bridle shiner	22	0.02
Central mudminnow	3	0.40	Black crappie	21	0.02
Northern pike	3	0.40	White perch	13	0.01
White perch	3	0.40	Banded killifish	10	0.01
Goldfish	2	0.27	Tadpole madtom	7	0.01
Cutlips minnow	1	0.13	Northern pike	5	0.01
Tadpole madtom	1	0.13	White catfish	4	0.00
White catfish	1	0.13	Goldfish	3	0.00

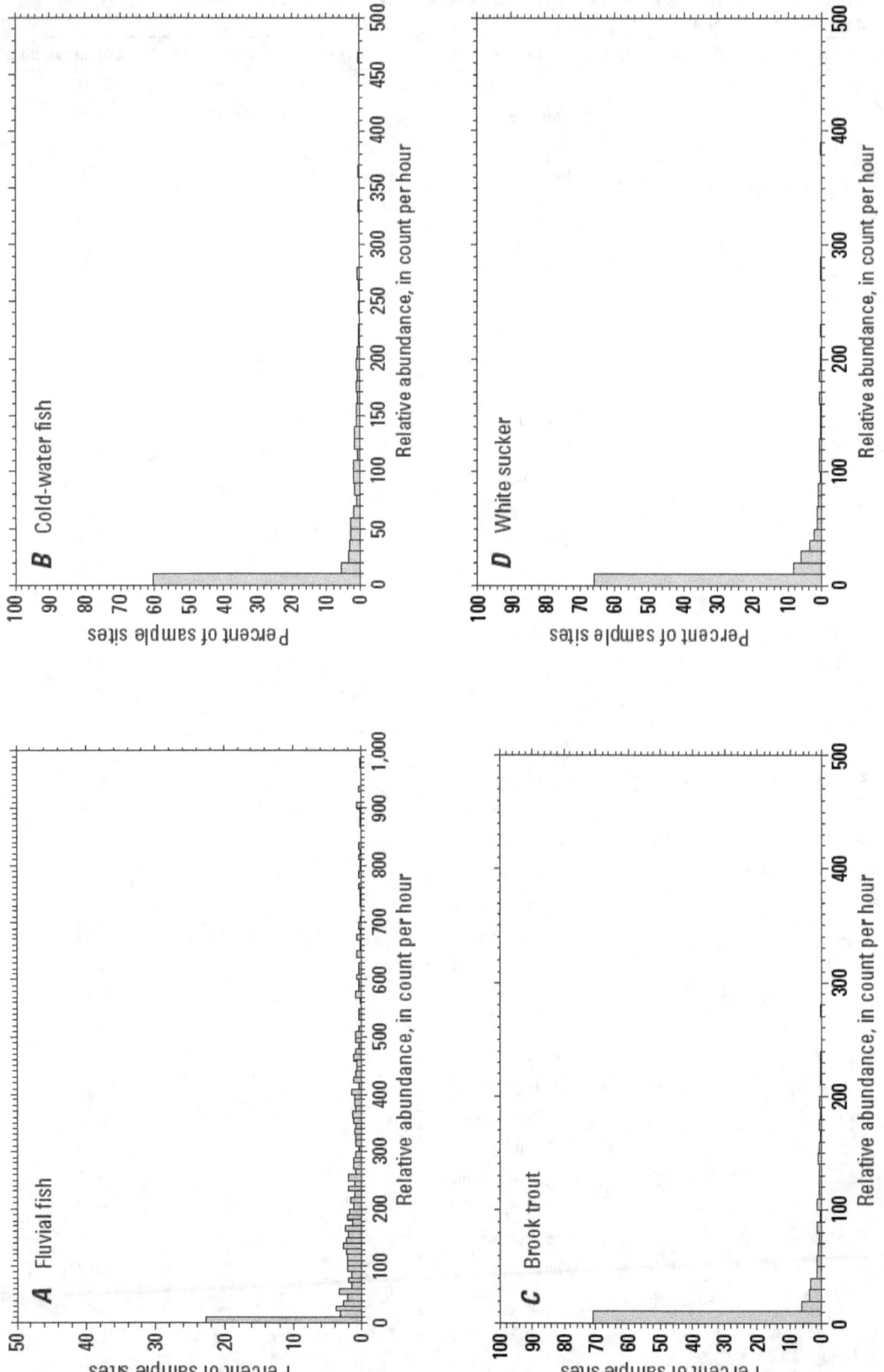

Figure 4.   Fish relative abundance in counts per hour of (*A*) fluvial fish, (*B*) cold-water fish, (*C*) brook trout, and (*D*) white sucker in relation to percent of selected sites in Massachusetts, 1998–2008.

fish metrics indicated that many distributions were highly non-normal and had a positive or right skew, with a majority of observations at or near zero values (fig. 4). For example, redbreast sunfish occurred at only 7 percent of the sites, and 24 other species occurred at even lower percentages of sites. Even the species that was present at the highest number of sites (white sucker), was absent at 48 percent of the sites. Pooling several species into fish-community metrics reduced the number of zero values. For example, fluvial fish occurred at 85 percent of the sampled sites.

Environmental Characteristics

Boxplots illustrate the range of environmental characteristics of the fish-sampling sites used in the study (fig. 5). The mean and median drainage areas were 28 and 7.4 mi^2, respectively, and drainage areas ranged from 2 to 395 mi^2. About 60 percent of the sample sites were in small basins less than 10 mi^2 in size, and roughly another 30 percent of sites were in basins of 10 to 50 mi^2. Less than 10-percent of the sites were in rivers with drainage areas greater than 50 mi^2. Summaries of environmental characteristics for the contributing areas to 756 fish-sampling sites in Massachusetts are presented in table 3. The sites represent a wide range of topographic, geologic, and land-cover conditions.

Boxplots illustrate the range of impervious cover and dam density at the fish-sampling sites used in the study (fig. 6). Dam density values ranged from 0 to 2.63 with a mean of 0.33 dams per square mile. Impervious-cover values ranged from 0.29 to 46 percent with mean and median values of 6.4 and 3.9 percent, respectively. A map of impervious cover for the fish-sampling sites used for this study indicates that the majority of sites that have an impervious cover greater than 12 percent are located in eastern and central Massachusetts (fig. 7). The degree and range of the percent impervious cover represented in the contributing areas to the 756 fish-sampling sites used in this study were compared to those reported in Weiskel and others (2010) for 1,429 subbasins and groundwater contributing areas in Massachusetts (fig. 8). The comparison indicated that the range and distribution of impervious cover for the sites used in this study are representative of impervious-cover values across Massachusetts or are only slightly underestimated.

Variables that are linearly related and highly correlated cannot be used together in a multivariable regression equation. Prior to analysis, all environmental characteristics and anthropogenic variables were evaluated for associations among variables through graphing and Pearson correlation analysis. A pairplot of environmental characteristics indicates that few variables have clear linear relations (fig. 9). A number of explanatory variables exhibit wedge-shaped scatter plots, indicating that there are clear limits for certain combinations of environmental characteristics for stream basins in Massachusetts. For example, few basins have both high basin slope and large areas of sand and gravel or wetlands.

Intercorrelations were expected and found among a few variables. Variables that exhibited a high degree of concordance (Pearson correlations, $r > 0.70$) were omitted or were not included in the same candidate models. For example, elevation was correlated with a number of variables including basin slope (0.72), sand and gravel (-0.72), and Outlet X (-0.88), and was omitted from further analysis. Outlet X was also correlated to basin slope (-0.75) but was retained for further evaluation during modeling. When a variable such as Outlet X is significant in regression equations, it can serve as a caution that correlation between response variables and explanatory variables is not equivalent to causation. For example, for fish species within their range of distribution, Outlet X does not in itself directly influence fish-community composition but likely covaries with multiple factors, such as gradient, climate, and land use. These factors, in turn, covary with unmeasured factors such as flow regime and velocity, water quality, and substrate conditions that directly influence fish distribution.

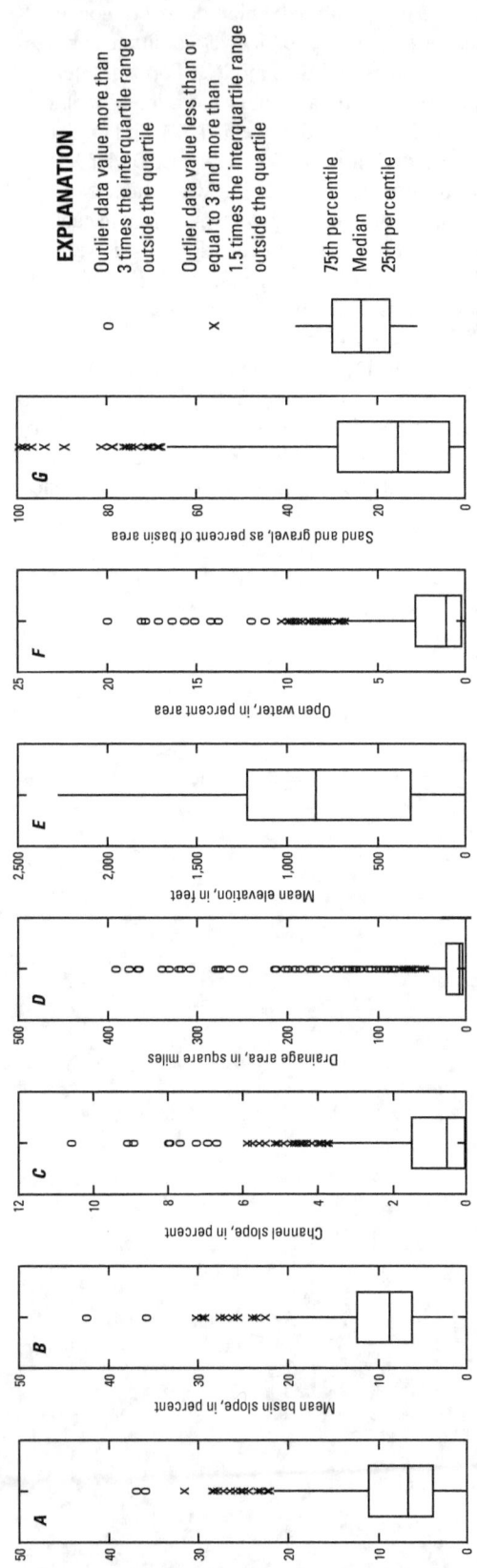

Figure 5. Environmental characteristics for contributing areas to 756 fish-sampling sites in Massachusetts (A) wetland area, (B) mean basin slope, (C) channel slope, (D) drainage area, (E) elevation, (F) open-water area, and (G) sand and gravel area.

Table 3. Descriptions, reference codes, units, number of sites, and ranges of values for environmental and anthropogenic variables.

Variable name	Code	Units	Number of sites	Minimum	Mean	25th percentile	Median	75th percentile	Maximum
Drainage area	DA	Square miles	756	2.0	27.7	3.7	7.4	22.7	394.5
Longitude	OutletX	State Plane meters/10000	756	0.3547	1.4953	0.9517	1.5310	1.9886	2.5880
Latitude	OutletY	State Plane meters/10000	756	8.1431	9.0384	8.8164	9.0873	9.2717	9.5800
Elevation	ELEV	Meters	756	41.0	832.8	316.5	839.3	1211.6	2272.1
Sand and gravel	SG	Percent area	756	0.0	20.6	3.5	15.4	28.9	100.0
Open water	OPENW	Percent area	756	0.0	2.2	0.2	1.1	2.9	20.1
Wetland	WET	Percent area	756	0.0	8.3	4.0	6.8	11.1	37.2
Channel slope	CHSLP	Percent rise	756	0.0	1.1	0.0	0.6	1.5	10.6
Basin slope	BASSLP	Percent rise	756	1.7	9.7	6.3	8.7	12.4	42.7
Impervious cover	IC	Percent area	756	0.3	6.4	1.9	3.9	8.9	46.2
Buffer impervious cover	BFIC	Percent area	749	0.0	5.2	2.1	3.8	6.6	39.8
Dam density	DamDsqmi	Count/square mile	749	0.00	0.33	0.00	0.26	0.49	2.63
Dam density	DamDstmi	Count/square mile	749	0.00	0.13	0.00	0.08	0.19	0.84
Percent alteration of August median for net Surcharged streams	AugPAsur	Percent	253	0.0	24.4	1.5	5.8	22.1	372.9
Percent alteration of August median for net Depleted streams	AugPAdep	Percent	503	-0.01	-9.8	-0.4	-0.9	-5.4	-100.0

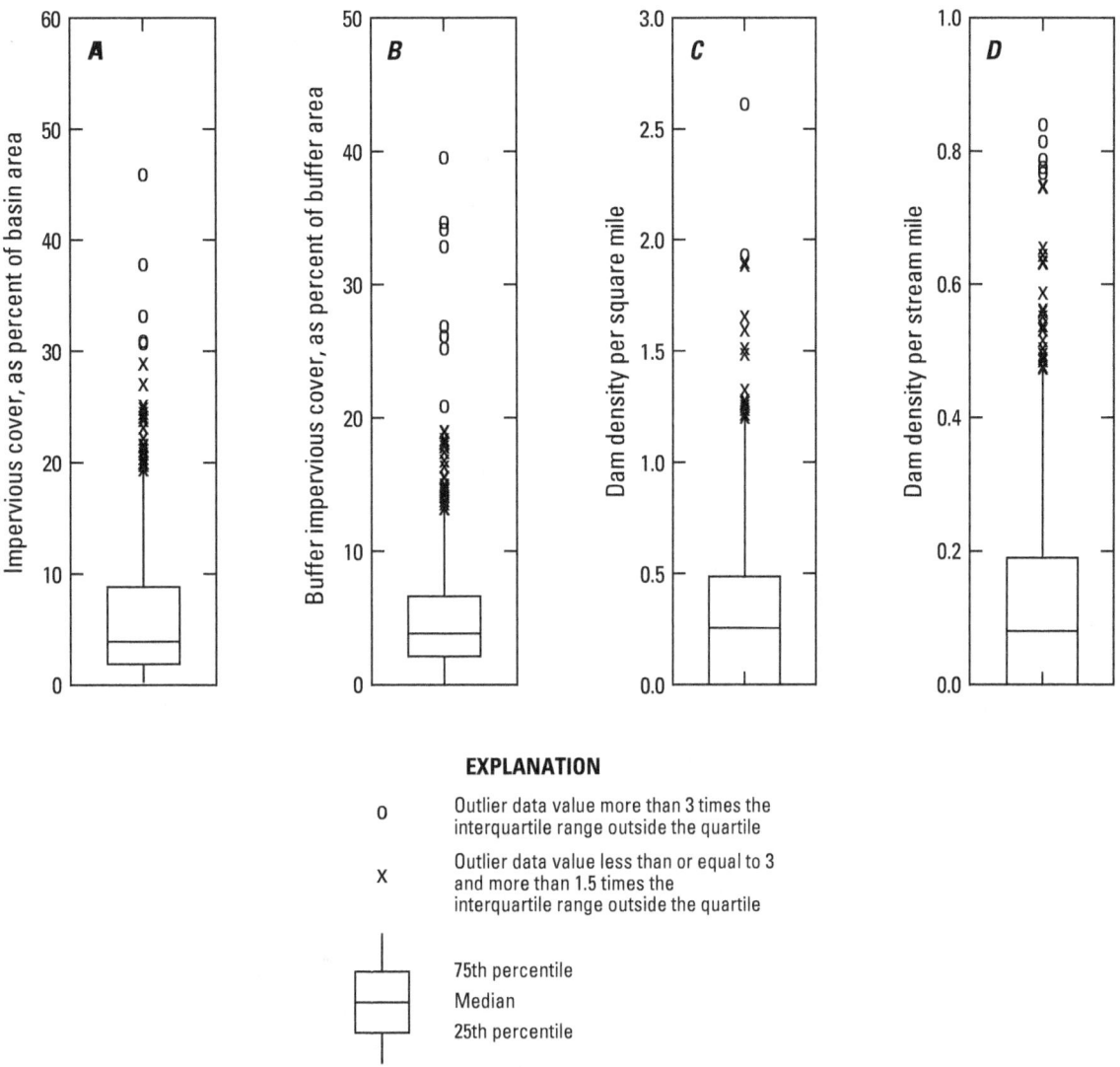

Figure 6. Anthropogenic characteristics for contributing areas to 756 fish-sampling sites in Massachusetts (*A*) impervious cover, (*B*) 240-meter-buffer impervious cover, (*C*) dam density per square mile, (*D*) dam density per stream mile.

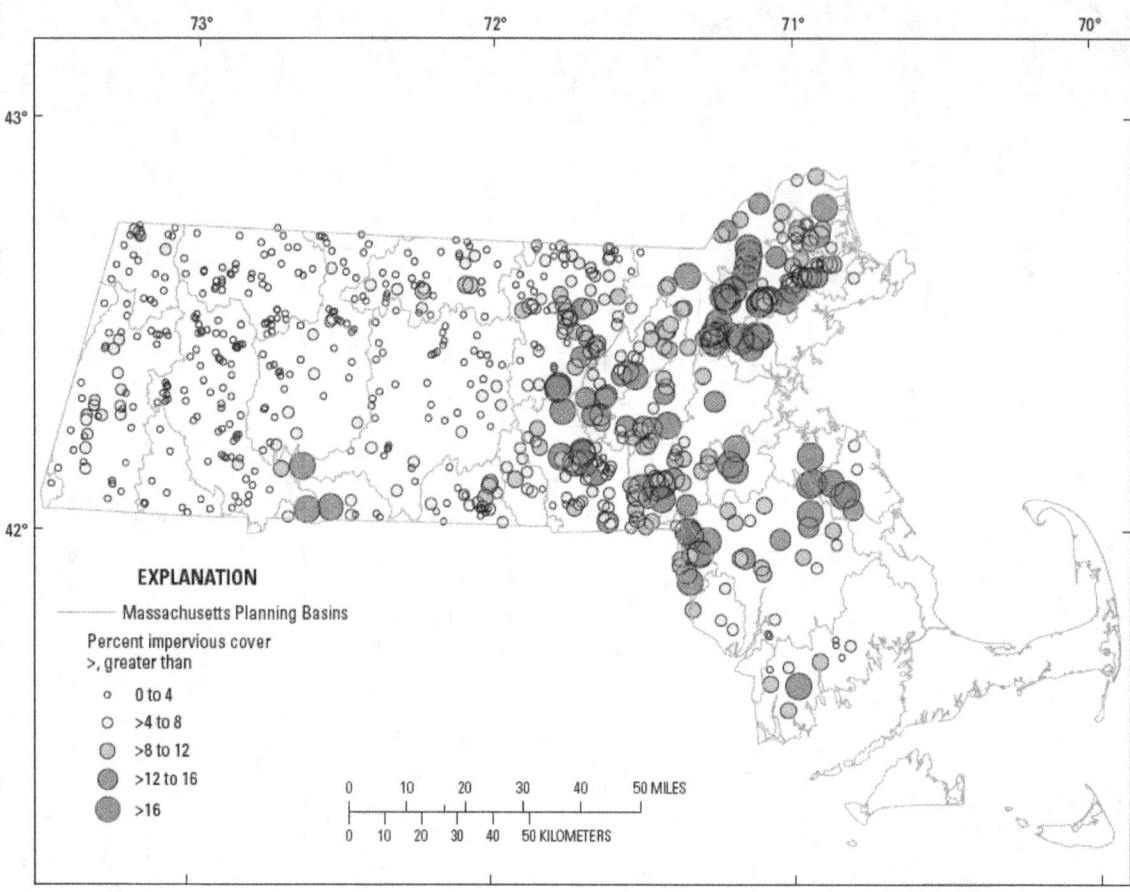

Figure 7. Impervious cover for contributing areas to 756 Massachusetts Division of Fisheries and Wildlife fish-sampling sites in Massachusetts, 1998–2008.

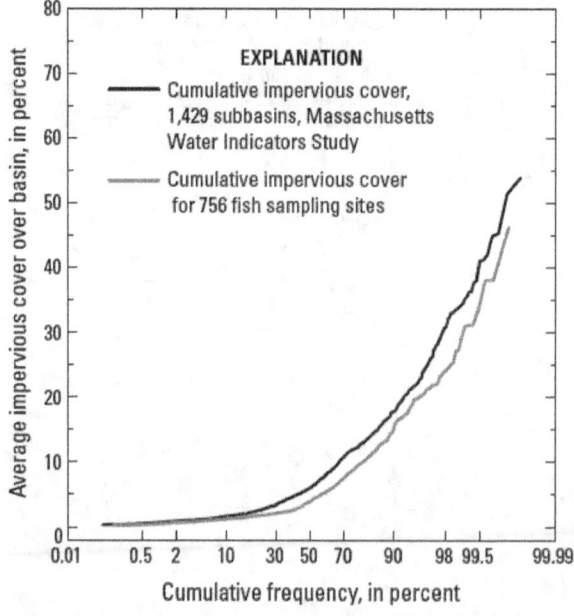

Figure 8. Frequency distributions of impervious cover for contributing areas to 756 Massachusetts Division of Fisheries and Wildlife fish-sampling sites and 1,429 subbasins and groundwater contributing areas across Massachusetts (Weiskel and others, 2010).

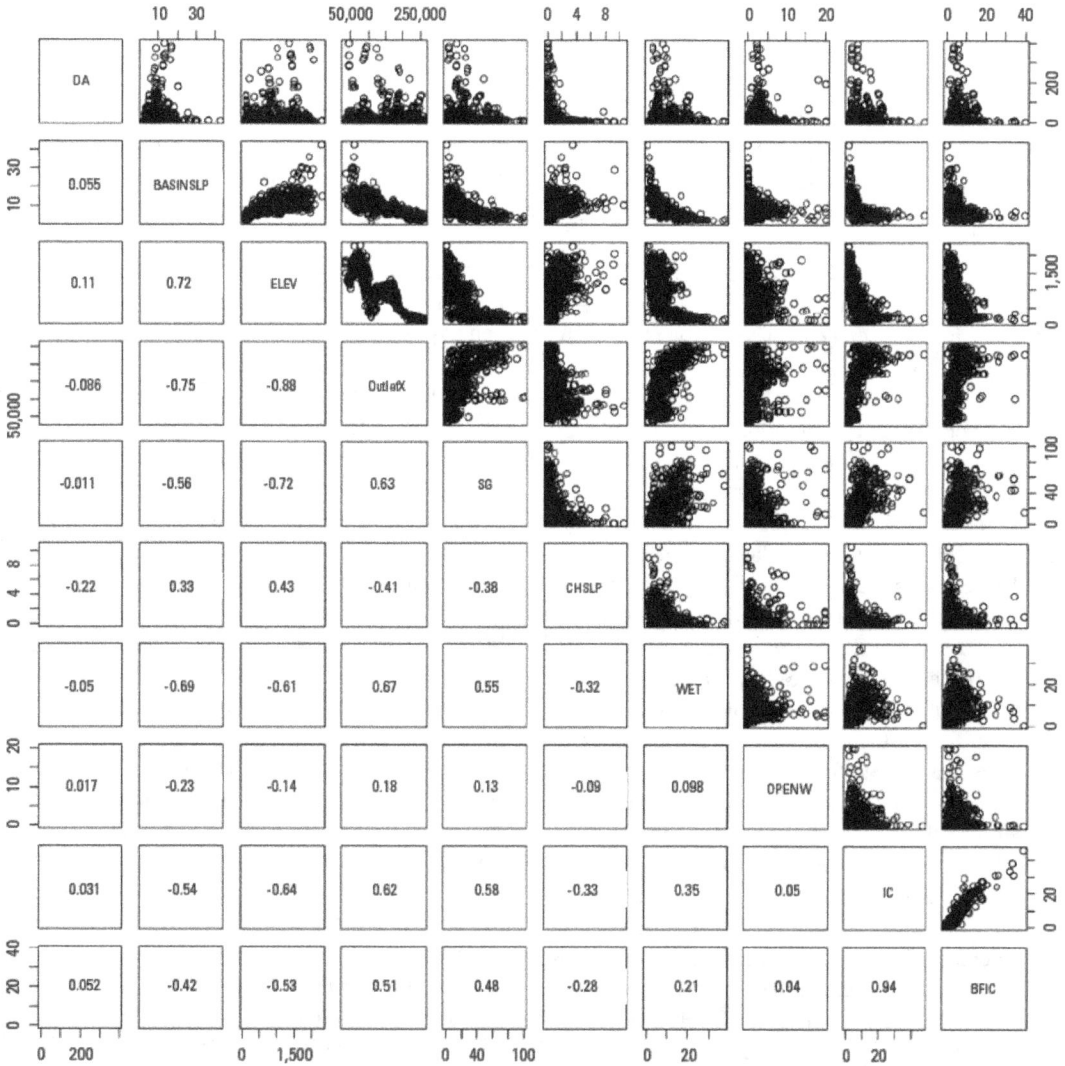

Figure 9. Pairplots of environmental characteristics. The lower diagonal panels show correlation values. The upper diagonal panels show pair-wise scatterplots. Names for environmental characteristics are given in table 3.

Quantile Regression

Quantile regression plots illustrate several trends in the limiting-factor relations between the fish-response variables and anthropogenic-alteration variables. For the plots shown, the direction of the slope of the 90th quantile indicates the nature of the relation. A quantile that decreases from left to right indicates a decrease in the fish-response variable in response to an increase in the stressor variable, and a quantile that increases from left to right indicates an increase in the fish variable in response to an increase in the stressor variable. The slope of the 90th-quantile line indicates the strength of the relation between the upper limit of the response variable and the stressor variable. A steeper line indicates a stronger relation between variables, and a flatter line indicates a weaker relation. The 95-percent confidence intervals around the 90th regression quantile lines indicate the uncertainty in the slope of the regression line. A narrow interval indicates a high degree of certainty; a wide interval indicates a lower degree of certainty. Confidence intervals that can encompass a line with a zero slope indicate that the relation between the two variables is insignificant.

Increases in the percent alteration of the August median flow for net-depleted sites were associated with large decreases in the 90th quantile for brook trout and blacknose dace relative abundance, slight declines in fallfish relative abundance, and little change in white sucker relative abundance (fig. 10). These trends are consistent with life history traits for the various species. Brook trout and blacknose dace are both fluvial specialists; the factor ceilings depicted by the 90th quantile support their sensitivity to flow alteration. The steep slope of the 90th quantile for brook trout and blacknose dace relative to other fluvial-fish species indicates that these species may be more sensitive to flow alteration than the other fluvial species tested. The low slope and wide confidence intervals of the regression lines for fallfish and white sucker indicate that, for this dataset, there is little to no relation between relative abundance of these species and percent alteration of August median flow for net-depleted sites.

Increases in percent alteration of August median flow for net-depleted sites were also associated with moderate declines for fluvial-fish relative abundance and species richness (fig. 11). The fluvial-fish-species-richness plot illustrates that for the 90th quantile, fluvial-fish species richness is reduced roughly one fluvial species by approximately a 16 percent reduction in August median flow.

Increases in the percent alteration of the August median flow for net-surcharged sites were associated with declines in the 90th quantile for relative abundance of blacknose dace, fallfish, and redfin pickerel (fig. 12). The wide confidence interval for brook trout indicates that, for this dataset, there is little to no relation between relative abundance of brook trout and percent alteration of August median flow at net-surcharged sites. There are relatively few sites with net-surcharge where brook trout were present, however, and the sample size may be too small to indicate the relation between net-surcharge and

brook trout relative abundance. Increases in the percent alteration of the August median flow for net-surcharged sites were associated with declines in the 90th quantile for the relative abundance of fluvial fish (fig. 13). The confidence intervals of the regression lines for fluvial-fish species richness indicate that, for this dataset, there is no relation between the number of fluvial fish species and percent alteration of August median flow for net-surcharged sites.

Increases in percent impervious cover were associated with large decreases in the 90th quantile for brook trout and blacknose dace, relatively little decline for fallfish, (fig. 14), and large decreases in the 90th quantile for fluvial-fish relative abundance and species richness (fig. 15). The declining relations shown in most of these plots illustrate the critical nature of the relations between impervious surface and aquatic condition. The narrow 95-percent confidence interval around the strongly declining relation between fluvial-fish species richness and impervious cover indicates a high degree of confidence in this relation. The effect of impervious cover has been hypothesized by Trebitz and others (2009) to be strong enough to mask other fish-habitat associations.

Relations between fish-response variables and impoundments were tested by use of a variable that reflects the areal size of impoundments, lakes, and ponds in the contributing area. Although some water bodies represented in this variable are natural lakes or ponds that do not have dams, many lakes and ponds in Massachusetts do have dams or outlet structures that control water levels. Increases in percent open water were associated with decreases in the 90th quantile for the relative abundance of fluvial fish, brook trout, and blacknose dace (fig. 16).

The quantile regression models are useful for modeling species responses to stressor gradients when those responses are linear, such as for the upper bound of a wedge-shaped relation. Although many of the relations between species responses and stressor gradients examined in this study exhibited a wedge shape, some scatter plots indicated a different form of relation. For example, relations between the relative abundance of redfin pickerel and percent alteration of August median flow, redfin pickerel and impervious cover, and white sucker and impervious cover, indicated nonlinear, unimodal responses that approximated a Gaussian (normal) curve (Gauch, 1982). Quantile regression models were not developed for these nonlinear relations for this preliminary study.

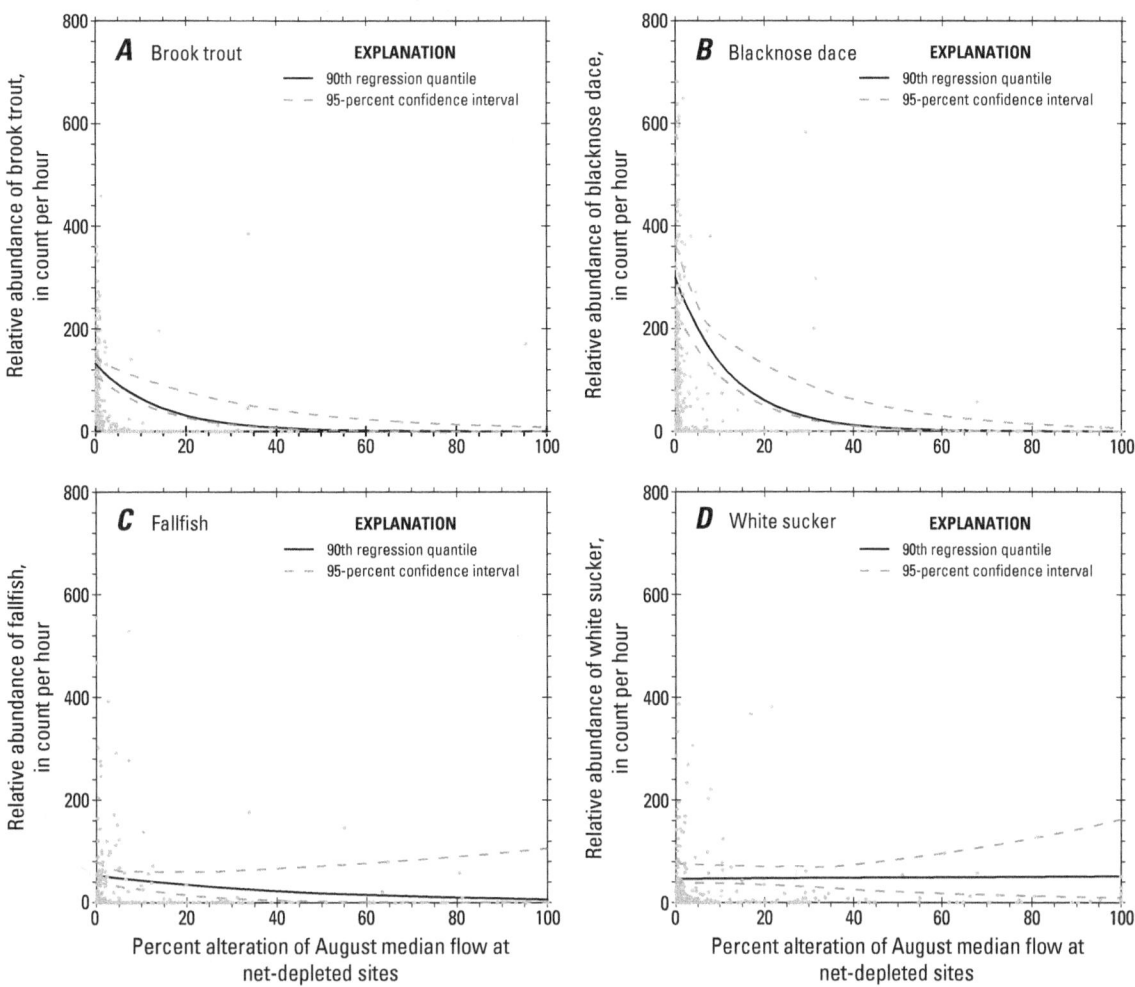

Figure 10. Relative abundance of indicator fish species in relation to percent alteration of August median flow at selected net-depleted sites for (*A*) brook trout, (*B*) blacknose dace, (*C*) fallfish, and (*D*) white sucker, in Massachusetts streams, 1998–2008.

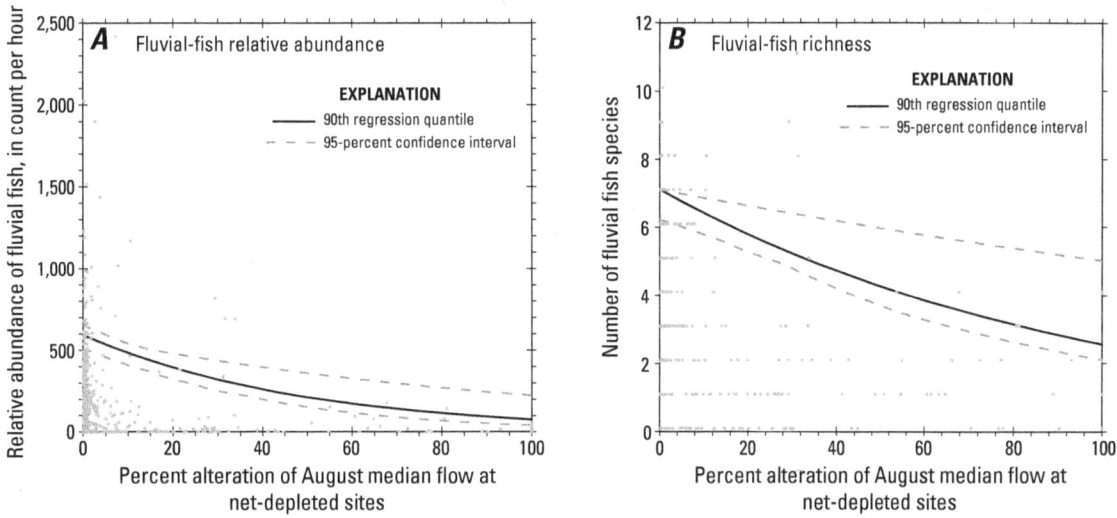

Figure 11. Fish-community metrics in relation to percent alteration of August median flow at selected net-depleted sites for (*A*) fluvial-fish relative abundance and (*B*) fluvial-fish species richness, in Massachusetts, 1998–2008.

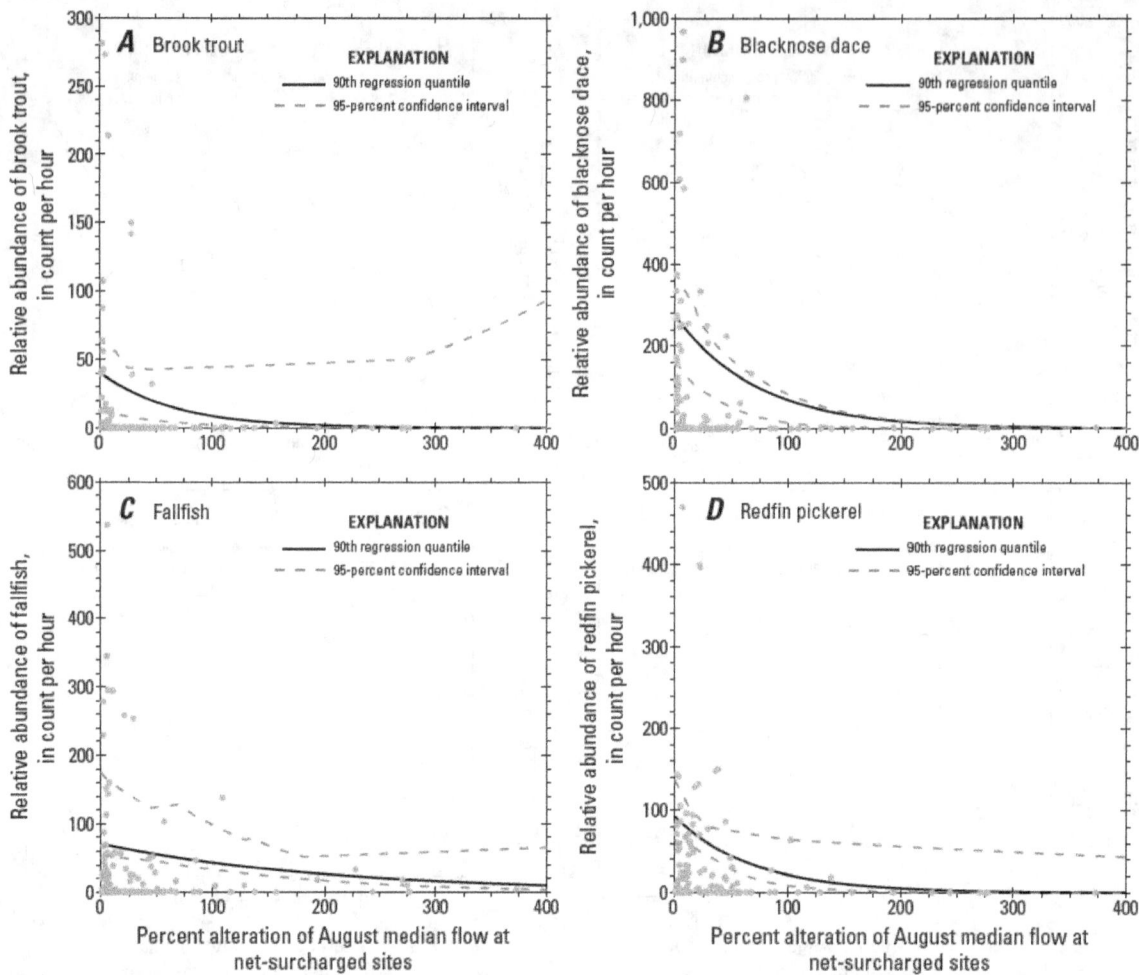

Figure 12.   Relative abundance of indicator fish species in relation to percent alteration of August median flow for selected net-surcharged sites for (*A*) brook trout, (*B*) blacknose dace, (*C*) fallfish, and (*D*) redfin pickerel, in Massachusetts streams, 1998–2008.

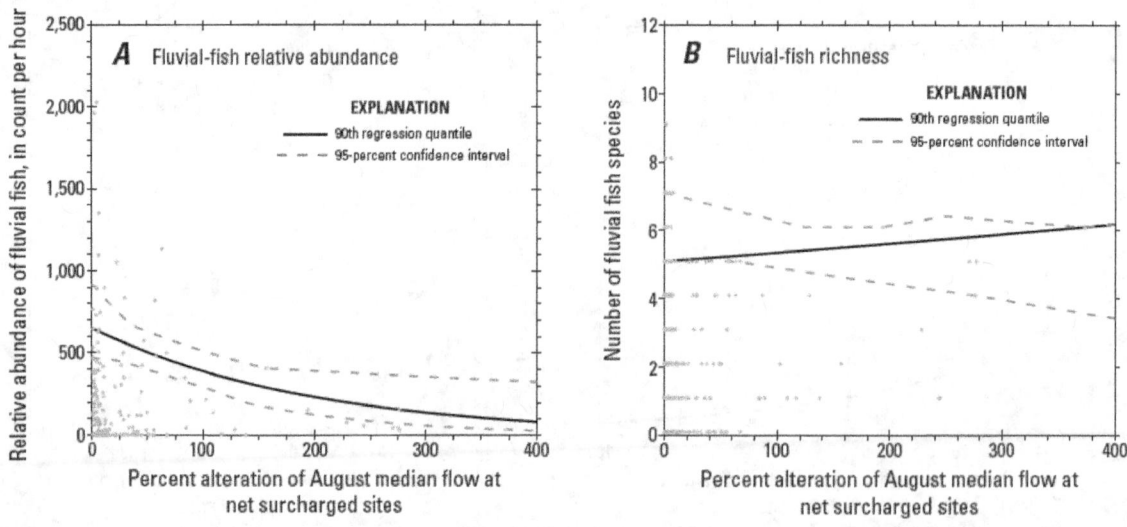

Figure 13.   Fish-community metrics in relation to percent alteration of August median flow at selected net-surcharged sites (*A*) fluvial-fish relative abundance, and (*B*) fluvial-fish species richness, in Massachusetts streams, 1998–2008.

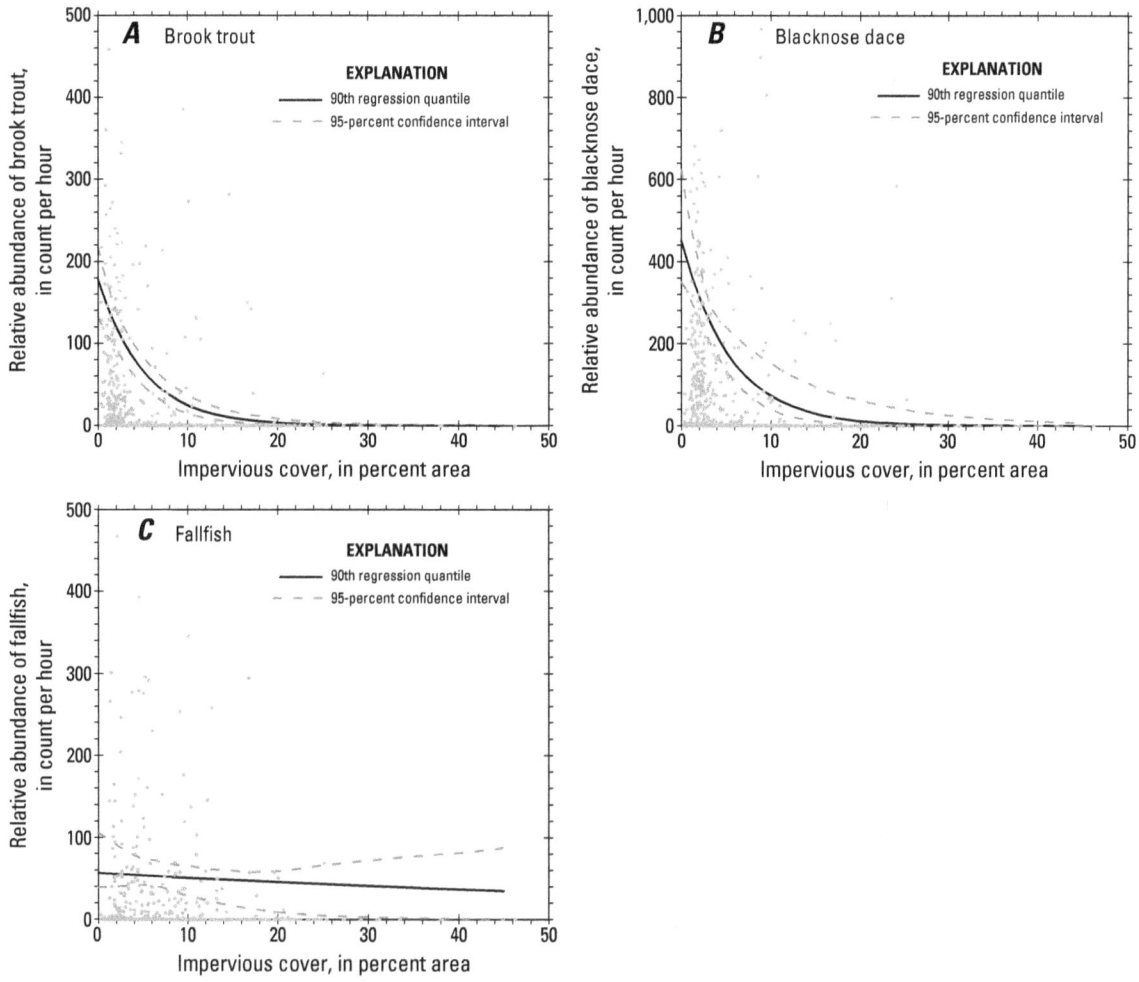

Figure 14.   Relative abundance of indicator-fish-species metrics in relation to impervious cover for (A) brook trout, (B) blacknose dace, and (C) fallfish, in selected Massachusetts streams, 1998–2008.

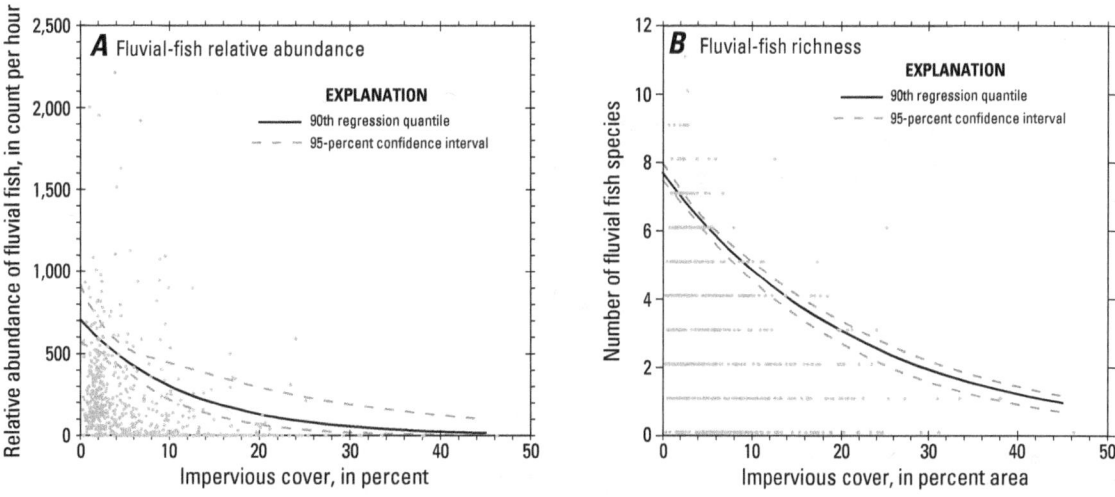

Figure 15.   Fish-community metrics in relation to impervious cover for (A) fluvial-fish relative abundance, and (B) fluvial-fish species richness, in selected Massachusetts streams, 1998–2008.

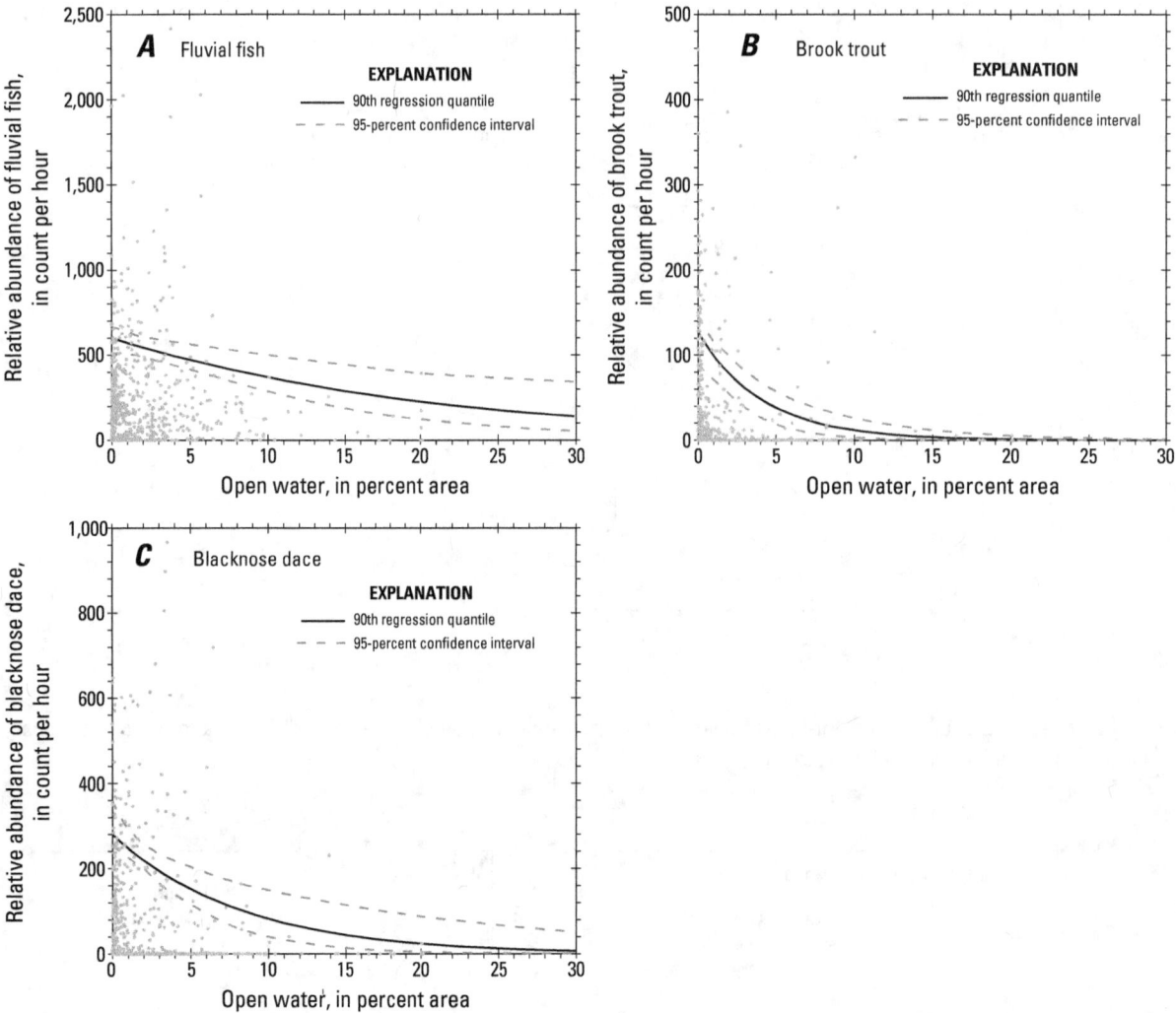

Figure 16.   Relative abundance of indicator-fish-species metrics in relation to open water for (*A*) fluvial fish, (*B*) brook trout, and (*C*) blacknose dace, in selected Massachusetts streams, 1998–2008.

Generalized Linear Models

Three GLM regression models were developed for this study—two for fish-community metrics (fluvial-fish relative abundance and fluvial-fish species richness) and one for an indicator-species metric (brook trout). Each of the models are described in the following sections, together with an example showing relations between variables. Additional plots depicting relations between all variables in the equations are presented later in the report.

The best-supported model for each of the fish-response variables was selected from the pool of potential explanatory variables on the basis of the candidate model with the smallest AIC. Significant variables and their coefficients for each regression equation are listed in table 4. The most commonly occurring variables are similar in all equations. Drainage area, channel slope, wetland area, impervious cover, and east-west location (Outlet X) occur in all three of the equations. The percent area of sand and gravel and the percent area of open water occur in the brook trout equation; two flow-alteration variables, percent alteration of August median flow and a variable indicating whether the site has either net-flow depletion or net-flow surcharge in August (DEPLAUG), each occur in the fluvial-fish relative-abundance equation.

Coefficients in the count and logistic portions of the GLM models are interpreted differently. Variable coefficients in the count portion of the model can be interpreted in the same way as coefficients from a multilinear OLS log-normal regression, provided those variables are not also present in the logistic part of the equation. For example, negative coefficients in the count portion of the fluvial-fish models indicate that an increase in that variable is associated with a decrease in fish abundance or species richness, and positive coefficients in the count portion of the models indicate that an increase in that variable is associated with an increase in fish abundance or species richness. The magnitude of the coefficient can be used to estimate the percent change in the response variable that is associated with a unit change in one covariate, keeping all other variables the same. The logistic portion of the equation models the probability of obtaining a zero in excess of any zeros expected from the count portion. This differs from a typical logistic regression that models the probability of occurrence. Positive coefficients in the logistic part of a ZINB model mean that an increase in that variable increases the probability that fish relative abundance or species richness will be zero. Because zeros can be generated by either the logistic process or the count process, interpretation of the magnitude of logistic coefficients is not straightforward. A graphical approach was used to examine the effect of a change in magnitude of a particular covariate on the response variable. Care should be taken in inferring cause and effect relations between response and explanatory variables. The equations should only be used to describe the current dataset.

The use of ZINB models is inappropriate for response variables that consist of percentages, such as percent fluvial fish. Response variables consisting of percentages can be fit with a GLM using a logit link. Logit GLMs fit with percent-fluvial fish data from this study were highly overdispersed because of a high number of points that contained 100-percent fluvial fish. Standard errors of individual coefficients were corrected to account for this overdispersion; however, the resulting models were still biased and deviance residuals were irregular, indicating a poor model fit. Nonparametric models or other multivariable statistical tools may be more appropriate for the percentage data, but time constraints limited testing their use for this study. The GLM regression models tested for coldwater fish and four additional indicator species (white sucker, blacknose dace, fallfish, and redfin pickerel) were either not significant at the 0.05 level compared to the null model, or exhibited extreme bias, and so were not included in this preliminary report.

Table 4. Significant variables and coefficients for generalized linear model equations used to determine relations between natural and anthropogenic factors and riverine-fish communities in Massachusetts. Independent variables and coefficients are for equation 3. Abbreviations for independent variables are given in table 3.

[SE, standard error; <, less than].

Model	Independent Variable for count process	Count process Coefficient (β_i)	SE	p-val	Independent Variable for logistic process	Logistic process Coefficient (γ_i)	SE	p-value
Fluvial-fish relative abundance	Intercept	7.7647	0.1929	<0.001	Intercept	-6.4089	0.8546	<0.001
	WET	-0.099	0.01	<0.001	DA	-0.1726	0.058	0.0029
	CHSLP	-0.096	0.0345	0.005	OutletX	3.2342	0.4218	<0.001
	DA	-0.0026	0.0009	0.0071				
	OutletX	-0.3228	0.1117	0.0038				
	IC	-0.057	0.0122	<0.001				
	AbsAugPA	-0.0044	0.0015	0.0035				
	DEPLAUG	-0.799	0.1206	<0.001				
Fluvial-fish species richness	Intercept	2.2092	0.0641	<0.001	Intercept	-5.0871	1.0201	<0.001
	WET	-0.0316	0.006	<0.001	DA	-0.4592	0.1507	0.0023
	CHSLP	-0.0974	0.0164	<0.001	OutletX	2.9988	0.4527	<0.001
	OutletX	-0.3955	0.0565	<0.001				
	IC	-0.0256	0.0059	<0.001				
Brook trout relative abundance	Intercept	4.561	0.0998	<0.001	Intercept	-4.0177	0.708	<0.001
	DA	-0.0744	0.006	<0.001	SG	-0.0309	0.0102	0.0025
					OPENW	0.2321	0.0571	<0.001
					WET	0.2399	0.0451	<0.001
					CHSLP	-0.5241	0.2093	0.0123
					OutletX	1.123	0.4265	0.0085
					IC	0.1306	0.0379	0.0006

Fluvial-Fish Species-Richness Model

Fluvial-fish species richness was related to percent wetland, channel slope, Outlet X, impervious surface, and drainage area. Species richness is negatively associated with percent wetland, channel slope, Outlet X, and impervious surface in the count part of the equation. Increases in these variables were associated with decreases in fluvial fish-species richness. The coefficients of the logistic part of the equation indicate that the probability of sampling fluvial-fish species increases for basins with larger drainage area and for basins in western MA. The coefficients for the fluvial fish-species richness model (table 4) can be used in equation 3 to determine the effect of changes in impervious cover on fluvial-fish species richness. Keeping all other variables static, a unit (1 percent) increase in impervious surface is associated with a 2.5 percent decrease in fluvial-fish species richness.

To illustrate relations between variables, the association between fluvial-fish species richness and impervious cover is depicted in figure 17 for four different levels of channel slope. These relations were determined with the fluvial-fish-species-richness equation, using the median values from the dataset for the environmental characteristics in the equation (drainage area, percent area of wetland, channel slope, Outlet X). On the plot, fluvial-fish species richness is shown to decrease with increasing impervious cover, and, for sites with low impervious cover, a site with a higher channel slope is indicated to have a lower expectation for fluvial-fish species richness (by one species) than a site with a lower channel slope.

Fluvial-Fish Relative-Abundance Model

Fluvial-fish relative abundance was related to percent wetland, channel slope, Outlet X, percent impervious cover, percent alteration of August median streamflow, and drainage area. The count portion of the equation indicated that fluvial-fish relative abundance is negatively associated with percent wetland, channel slope, Outlet X, percent impervious cover, and percent alteration of August median streamflow. The coefficients in the logistic portion of the model indicate that the probability of sampling fluvial fish increases for basins with larger drainage areas and for basins in western MA. The coefficients for the fluvial-fish-relative-abundance model (table 4) can be used in equation 3 to determine the effect of changes in flow alteration on fluvial-fish relative abundance. Keeping all other variables static, a unit increase in impervious surface is associated with a 5.5-percent decrease in fluvial-fish relative abundance. Keeping all other variables static, a unit increase in percent alteration of August median streamflow is associated with a 0.4-percent decrease in fluvial-fish relative abundance for net-depleted or for net-surcharged streams. The equation also included a variable (DEPLAUG) that indicates there is a difference in the relative abundance of fluvial fish between streams that have net-depleted and those that have net-surcharged conditions. Streams with net-depleted conditions have about 55-percent fewer fish than streams with net-surcharged stream conditions.

The association between fluvial-fish relative abundance and flow alteration is depicted in figure 18 for net-depleted and

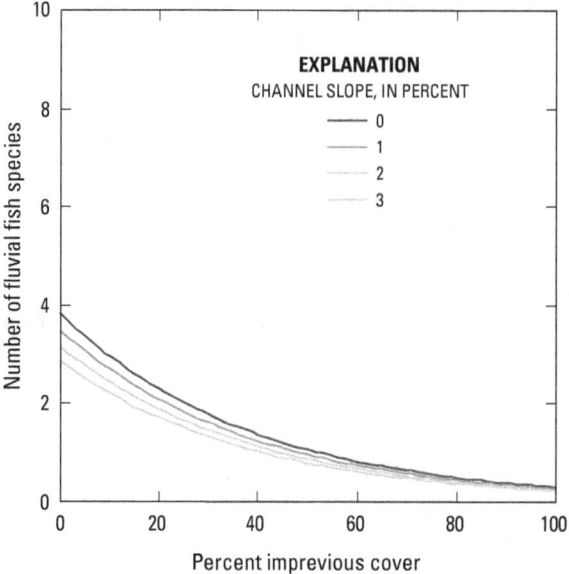

Figure 17. Generalized linear model output for relations among fluvial-fish species richness, percent impervious cover, and channel slope, in selected Massachusetts streams, 1998–2008.

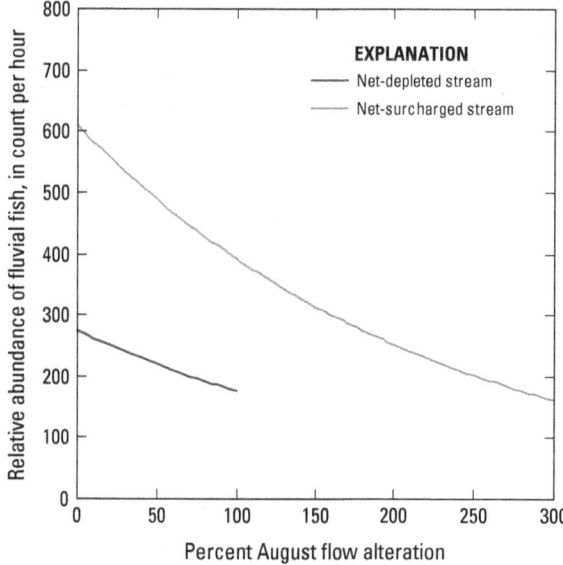

Figure 18. Generalized linear model output for relations between fluvial-fish relative abundance and percent alteration of August median flow for selected net-depleted and net-surcharged streams in Massachusetts, 1998–2008.

net-surcharged streams under median August conditions. For illustration, these relations were determined with the fluvial-fish relative-abundance equation, using the median values from the dataset for the environmental characteristics, and setting the percent impervious cover value to zero.

Brook Trout Relative-Abundance Model

Brook trout relative abundance was related to impervious cover, channel slope, Outlet X, percent area of sand and gravel, open water, and wetland. The count part of the equation indicates that brook trout relative abundance decreases with increasing drainage area. Coefficients from the logistic portion of the equation indicate that brook trout are more likely to occupy basins with a high percent area of sand and gravel, low percent area of open water, low percent area of wetland, high channel slopes, low percent impervious cover, and basins in western Massachusetts (table 4). The coefficients of the logistic part of the brook trout relative-abundance equation indicate that increasing impervious cover decreases the probability of brook trout in a stream.

Although the brook trout equation did not contain a flow-alteration variable, this does not necessarily indicate that brook trout are unaffected by flow alterations. Three other variables in the brook trout equation—percent sand and gravel, percent open water, and percent impervious cover—can each be considered to encompass a streamflow aspect. For example, increases in impervious cover have been demonstrated to be associated with increased flashiness

and increased temperatures, and increases in impoundments (percent open water) may also result in flow alterations and increased temperatures. The percent area of sand and gravel tends to be positively correlated with baseflow; the presence of sand and gravel in the brook trout equation supports the assumption that high baseflows and associated cool stream temperatures are important factors for brook trout. The association between brook trout relative abundance and impervious cover is depicted in figure 19 for different percent areas of sand and gravel. These relations were determined with the brook trout relative-abundance equation, using the median values from the dataset for the environmental characteristics. The relations shown on the plot indicate that brook trout relative abundance does not initially decline as quickly (in response to increased impervious cover) in basins with a high percent area of sand and gravel as it does in basins with a low percent area of sand and gravel, indicating the importance of maintaining groundwater discharge to support cold-water fish communities in streams in developing areas.

Model Validation and Limitations

Predicted values from a remove-one cross validation were compared to observed values for each fitted GLM (table 5). Correlation coefficients for the fitted models ranged from 0.42 to 0.65, indicating a low-to-moderate correlation between observed and predicted values of fluvial-fish relative abundance and species richness. These values were within reported ranges for ecological models (Potts and Elith, 2006; Pearce and Ferrier, 2001). The equations for fluvial-fish species richness and fluvial-fish relative abundance had the best fit, with correlation coefficients of 0.65 and 0.54, respectively. In addition, for the fluvial-fish species-richness model, the intercept of the linear regression line between observed and predicted values was not significantly different from 0, and the slope was not different from 1, indicating that predictions from the fluvial-fish-species-richness equation are relatively unbiased. The fluvial-fish relative-abundance model had a lower proportion of the variability explained than the fluvial-fish species-richness model, and a plot of the model-predicted versus observed data indicated that the fluvial-fish relative-abundance equation slightly overpredicts the relative abundance of fluvial fish for sites with high abundance. All three of the models were significant at the 0.05 level compared to the null model (intercept only).

Statistical models of species abundance often fail to produce consistently reliable predictions (Pearce and Ferrier, 2001). The measures of model validation in table 5 indicate that the models in this study have a low-to-moderate predictive capability, although they are within the range of reported values for ecological models (Pearce and Ferrier, 2001; Potts and Elith, 2006; Meador and Carlisle, 2009; Roy and others, 2009; Snelder and Lamouroux, 2010). Poor model performance may be attributed to many causes, including unmeasured factors, the choice of environmental characteristics and anthropogenic covariates tested, location of sample sites

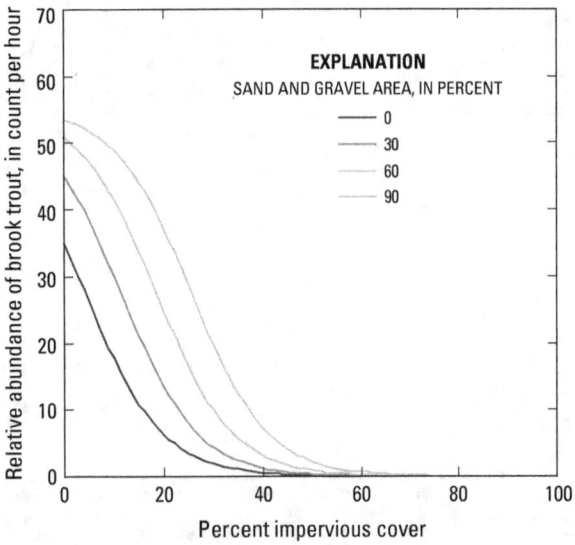

Figure 19. Generalized linear model output for relations among brook trout relative abundance, percent impervious cover, and percent area sand and gravel, in selected Massachusetts streams, 1998–2008.

Figure 5. Measures of goodness of fit for comparisons of observed and predicted values for generalized linear model equations for fluvial-fish richness, fluvial-fish relative abundance, and brook trout relative abundance.

[Pearson's r, Pearson's correlation coefficient; CI, confidence interval]

Model	Pearson's r	intercept	95-percent CI for intercept	Slope	95-percent CI for slope
Fluvial-fish relative abundance	0.54	33.07	22.63 to 43.49	0.55	0.48 to 0.61
Fluvial-fish richness	0.65	0.00	-0.28 to 0.28	1	0.92 to 1.08
Brook trout relative abundance	0.42	-3.78	-11.20 to 3.63	1.22	1.02 to 1.40

relative to alterations, errors in determining environmental predictors from a GIS, fish-capture efficiency, and the use of modeled rather than measured flow data. For example, although there may be significant relations between fish abundance and species richness and basin-scale characteristics such as drainage area and percent wetland, fish do not occupy an entire basin with equal frequency. Use of data concerning local-scale variables, such as site-specific habitat, stream-flow, and stream characteristics, may help to improve model performance. Without accounting for many other factors that influence fish communities and that were unmeasured for this study, such as stream temperature, water quality, and site-specific streamflow measurements, it may be difficult to develop equations that have substantially higher model performance.

Several issues need to be addressed to assist with interpretation of the models. The first is that fish-response variables do not necessarily drop to zero when simulated August median flows reach 100-percent depletion. One confounding factor is that fish-community sampling does not take place in dry streambeds, and so one extreme end of the spectrum of environmental alteration is missing from the dataset. A corollary to this is that streams were sampled during a period, month, or year when the flow was not zero. In addition, the condition could arise where the simulated SYE streamflows, which reflect overall water use, may not necessarily represent instantaneous streamflows. The SYE streamflows reflect daily flows modeled over a 45-year period, using water-use values that are determined from annual water-use data that is averaged over a 5-year period, disaggregated into monthly water use by use of a simulated demand curve, and further disaggregated into daily water use (Weiskel and others, 2010). In contrast, the fish-sample information came from a single sample collected in a single day. In the model, 100-percent depletion of August median flow would only correspond to dry streambeds for times when the median (or less) flow was present in the stream channel. If flows are higher than the August median, water withdrawals would still leave some (reduced) streamflow. Although fluvial-fish relative abundance does not, on average, drop to zero for simulated 100-percent depletion of August median flow, the likelihood of zero values for fluvial fish does increase. For example, the 100 samples with the lowest August depletion included only 6 zero values for fluvial fish relative abundance, and the 100 samples with the highest August alteration included 24 zero values.

A second issue to consider when interpreting the models is that the range over which a fish variable responds should be considered the sensitivity of this variable to the explanatory variables. For example, if the fluvial-fish relative abundance at a given level of watershed size, wetland area, slope, impervious cover and range of August median flow depletion ranges from a relative abundance of 275 to 125, the variable is only responsive over 150 units. In other words, an alteration of 150 units of fluvial-fish relative abundance in this example would be equivalent to 100 percent of the response.

Each of the GLM equations do not necessarily contain all of the anthropogenic-stressor variables that were tested. For example, the fluvial-fish species-richness and brook trout relative-abundance models do not contain flow alteration variables, and the fluvial-fish species-richness and fluvial-fish relative-abundance models do not contain a measure of impoundments or dam density. Although this indicates that for this dataset, a strong relation between these explanatory variables and the mean values for the fish community measures was not detected, it does not necessarily indicate that there is no relation between these factors and fish communities. For some variables, the quantile regression plots indicate relations between fish community measures and explanatory variables that were not depicted by the GLM equations. For example figure 10B indicates a declining relation between fluvial-fish species richness and percent alteration of August median flow, and figure 16A indicates a declining relation between the relative abundance of fluvial fish and the percent area of open water.

Fish-Community Response to Flow Alteration and Impervious Cover

The multivariable relations between any two explanatory variables and a fish-response variable can be examined by generating a plot from the GLM equations showing a series of lines (or family of curves). Figures 20–22 (back of report) show families of curves for each of the three GLM equations. In these figures, fish response is plotted against the anthropogenic-alteration variables that are in the various equations, such as impervious cover or flow alteration. By varying a second, environmental characteristic variable in the equation in conjunction with the stressor variable, a family of curves can be drawn depicting the fish-metric response. For example, figures 21A-D show families of curves indicating the response of the relative abundance of fluvial fish to impervious cover, using the median values from the dataset for the environmental characteristics in the equation. For the fluvial-fish relative-abundance equation, a unit increase in impervious surface is associated with a 5.5-percent decrease in fluvial-fish relative abundance, keeping other variables constant. This association is held across all values of other explanatory variables. However, the maximum expected value for fluvial-fish relative abundance decreases when the channel slope or percent wetland is increased, producing a slightly different curve. Other variables on the fluvial-fish relative-abundance plots indicate less of a response. For example, a unit increase in drainage area does not result in large changes in the relative abundance of fluvial fish.

The GLM equations could be used to develop families of curves for any characteristics for which appropriate information is available and used to illustrate the relative response of fluvial-fish species richness, and the relative abundance of fluvial fish and brook trout, to alteration while setting different initial expectations using environmental characteristics. For example, the equations could be used to assess the drainage area-size classes or gradient classes of various classification frameworks, such as the Northeast Aquatic Habitat Classification (Gawler and others, 2008; Olivero and others, 2008), for the particular variables that are in the equations. Another potential application could be to apply the regression equation statewide, for example, to each of the 1,429 sub basins delineated in the Massachusetts Water Indicators project (Weiskel and others, 2010). All variables for the GLM equations are available from the Massachusetts Water Indicators project, with the exception of local channel slope, which could be calculated. Once the equation has been run with the existing conditions (current impervious cover and flow alteration), expected reference conditions could be developed by setting the impervious cover and flow alteration metrics to zero or some least-altered value, and holding all other variables constant.

The GLM model predictions represent the mean response at a given site. Stochastic processes make it difficult to predict abundance at a site with a high degree of precision, however. For a given reach, there is a high degree of temporal variability in abundance data. For any application of the models it is important to note that the various models only account for 42 to 65 percent of the variability, as measured by the correlation between observed and predicted values, and particular caution is needed when extrapolating to the extremes of any one variable. For example, because very few fish-community measurements were made at sites having zero or over 20 percent impervious cover, the model is less robust at these ends of the impervious-cover spectrum. Consequently, these models are best employed to compare fish-community response among a set of sites or to look at the change in the mean response associated with a change in a particular covariate. Although the predictive ability is low to moderate in these models, the

relations characterized by the coefficients in the model are highly significant. In a model with relatively little bias, these relations can be used to examine how fish-response variables change along a gradient of values for a particular explanatory variable.

Suggestions for Further Study

The explanatory power of the GLM models can potentially be improved by identifying additional attributes to test while developing new equations. For example, the dam-density measure used to represent the effect of impoundments was determined not to be a significant variable for this dataset, even though research has indicated a link to this variable in the literature (Wenger and others, 2008). Although dam density in a watershed is easy to calculate and might be highly correlated to pooled fisheries information (for example, all the fish sites in a watershed for which dam density is calculated), other measures, such as counts of dams, distance to a dam, or length of river free of dams, may be better correlated to changes in fish-response variables at a given site (Wang and others, 2010). Stream temperature has also been determined to be a important variable for determining fish distribution and abundance (Zorn and others, 2009). These additional variables could be tested.

The diversity of the responses of individual fluvial-fish species to flow alteration and impervious cover highlights the importance of a species-by-species analysis in addition to evaluating fish-community metrics. Though a number of species can be classified in a similar fashion (for example, fluvial), this does not necessarily indicate that each species will respond in the same way to environmental variables or anthropogenic stresses. An *a priori* classification of fish, such as fluvial specialist or fluvial dependent, although intuitive, might homogenize responses and reduce the ability to detect the magnitude and direction of response. Assignments of each species to the habitat-use classifications used in this report were made on the basis of life-history traits and best professional judgment (Bain and Meixler, 2008; Kashiwagi and Richards, 2009). Additional tools like Threshold Indicator Taxa ANalysis (TITAN) (Baker and King, 2010; King and Baker, 2010) could be used to determine the nature of response of each species to various stressor gradients. TITAN analyses describe how individual species respond along a particular gradient (for example, impervious cover) and allow direct comparisons of the direction and extent of the response. Species that respond similarly could potentially be combined into community classes by grouping species that respond similarly (increasers or decreasers) to different stressor variables.

Summary

Fish-sampling data for 756 Massachusetts Fisheries and Wildlife fish-sampling sites were used to determine a set of fish-community and indicator-species variables. A review of the literature was used to select a set of fish-community variables thought to be responsive to flow alteration, along with a set of environmental and anthropogenic variables considered to be important for determining fish abundance and distribution. Fish-community metrics selected for testing as response variables include relative abundance, species richness, and percent of fluvial fish and cold-water fish. Individual fish-species-response variables tested included relative abundance of brook trout, blacknose dace, fallfish, redfin pickerel, and white sucker. Contributing areas to the fish-sampling sites were determined using a Geographic Information System (GIS), and a selected set of environmental characteristics and anthropogenic-alteration variables were determined for each fish-sampling site for use as explanatory variables. Environmental characteristics tested included basin slope, channel slope, elevation, percent sand and gravel, percent wetland, percent open water, and site location. Anthropogenic variables tested included flow alteration, impervious cover, and dam density. Flow-alteration metrics used in the study were determined from streamflows simulated for each fish-sampling site using the USGS Sustainable Yield Estimator (Archfield and others, 2010). Indicators of flow alteration tested were consistent with those used for the USGS Massachusetts Water Indicators report (Weiskel and others, 2010), and included percent alteration of August median flow, water use intensity, and the withdrawal and return-flow fraction of streamflow. Bivariate scatter plots of many relations between species and anthropogenic alterations have a wedge shape, indicating a heterogeneous variance and a strong right skew. The declining upper edge of a wedge-shaped relation can indicate that an explanatory variable can act as a constraint on organisms. Quantile regression was used to fit 90th regression quantiles to characterize this upper edge for selected fish-response variables. Results of quantile regression indicate that flow alteration and impervious cover are negatively associated with both fluvial-fish relative abundance and fluvial-fish species richness and that percent area of open water is negatively associated with fluvial-fish relative abundance. The strength of the response varied by species.

Generalized linear models (GLMs) were used to relate a suite of explanatory variables to the selected fish-response variables. GLMs are the appropriate analytical tool for non-normally distributed data, count data, and datasets with large numbers of zero values. Numerous models were tested. The three strongest models included those for fluvial-fish species richness, fluvial-fish relative abundance, and brook trout relative abundance. The variables in the equations were demonstrated to be significant ($p < 0.05$, with most < 0.01). The amount of variability in fish-response variables that could be attributed to anthropogenic alterations and environmental characteristics by the equations was low to moderate. Correlation coefficients between observed and predicted values of the fitted models range from 0.42 to 0.65, but these values are in line with those reported in the literature for similar studies.

Impervious cover and flow alteration both were demonstrated to influence fish communities, and the equations were used to quantify the change in fish-community metrics associated with a unit change in flow alteration and imperviousness. The fluvial-fish-species-richness equation indicated that, keeping all other variables the same, a unit increase in impervious surface is associated with a 2.5-percent decrease in fluvial-fish species richness. The fluvial-fish relative-abundance equation indicated that, keeping all other variables the same, a unit increase in percent alteration of August median streamflow in net-depleted streams or net-surcharged streams is associated with a 0.4-percent decrease in relative abundance of fluvial fish. Streams with net-depleted conditions have about 55-percent fewer fish than streams with net-surcharged stream conditions. Keeping all other variables the same, a unit increase in impervious surface is associated with a 5.5-percent decrease in fluvial-fish relative abundance. The brook trout relative-abundance equation indicated that an increase in impervious cover decreases the probability of brook trout presence in a stream. Brook trout relative abundance does not initially decline as quickly (in response to increased impervious cover) in basins with a high percent area of sand and gravel as it does in basins with a low percent area of sand and gravel, indicating the importance of maintaining groundwater discharge to support cold-water fish communities in streams in developing areas.

The GLM equations were used to illustrate multivariable relations between fish-response variables and explanatory variables by developing a family of curves for the model equations by changing the value for one variable and holding all other variables constant. The relations and equations can be used as a tool to help assess the potential fish responses to different water- and land-management decisions for small- to medium-sized streams in Massachusetts. The models can be used to illustrate statewide relations between fish-community metrics and anthropogenic and environmental variables.

References Cited

Aumadi-Nedushan, Behrouz, St-Hilaire, Andre, Berrube, Michel, Robichaud, Elaine, Thiemonge, Nathalie, and Bobee, Bernard, 2006, A review of statistical methods for the evaluation of aquatic habitat suitability for Instream flow assessment: River Research and Applications, v. 22, p. 503–523.

Akaike, H., 1974, A new look at the statistical model identification: IEEE Transactions on Automatic Control, v. 19, p. 716–723.

Anderson, M.J., 2008, Animal-sediment relationships re-visited—characterizing species distributions along an environmental gradient using canonical analysis and quantile regression splines: Journal of Experimental Marine Biology and Ecology: v. 366, p. 16–27

Angermeier, P.L., and Karr, J.L., 1986, Applying an index of biotic integrity based on stream-fish communities—considerations in sampling and interpretation: American Journal of Fisheries Management, v. 6, p. 418–429.

Annear, T., Chisholm, I., Beecher, H., Locke, A., and 12 other authors, 2004, Instream Flows for Riverine Resource Stewardship: Cheyenne, Wyoming, Instream Flow Council revised edition, 268 p.

Arab, A., Wildhaber, M.L., Wikle, C.K., and Gentry, C. N., 2008, Zero-inflated modeling of fish catch per unit area resulting from multiple gears: Application to channel catfish and shovelnose sturgeon in the Missouri River: North American Journal of Fisheries Management, v. 28, p. 1044–1058.

Archfield, S.A., Vogel, R.M., Steeves, P.A., Brandt, S.L., Weiskel, P.K., and Garabedian, S.P., 2010, The Massachusetts Sustainable-Yield Estimator—a decision-support tool to assess water availability at ungaged stream locations in Massachusetts: U.S. Geological Survey Scientific Investigations Report 2009-5227, 41 p.

Argent, D.G., Bishop, J.A., Stauffer, J.R., Carline, R.F., and Myers W.L., 2003, Predicting freshwater fish distributions using landscape-level variables: Fisheries Research, v. 60, p. 17–32.

Armstrong, D.S., Parker, G.W., and Richards, T.A., 2008, Characteristics and classification of least altered streamflows in Massachusetts: U.S. Geological Survey Scientific Investigations Report 2007-5291, 113 p.

Armstrong, D.S., Parker, G.W., and Richards, T.A., 2004, Evaluation of streamflow requirements for habitat protection by comparison to streamflow characteristics at index streamflow-gaging stations in southern New England: U.S. Geological Survey Water-Resources Investigations Report 03-4332, 101 p.

Armstrong, D.S., Richards, T.A., and Parker, G.W., 2001, Assessment of habitat, fish communities, and streamflow requirements for habitat protection, Ipswich River, Massachusetts, 1998–99: U.S. Geological Survey Water-Resources Investigations Report 01-4161, 72 p.

Arthington, A.A., Bunn, S.E., Poff, N.L., and Naiman, R.J., 2006, The challenge of providing environmental flow rules to sustain river ecosystems: Ecological Applications, v. 16, no. 4, p. 1311–1318.

Austin, Mike, 2007, Species distribution models and ecological theory—a critical assessment and some possible new approaches: Ecological Modelling, v. 200, p. 1–19.

Bain, M.B., Finn, J.T., and Booke, H.E., 1988, Streamflow regulation and fish community structure: Ecology, v. 69, no. 2, p. 382–392.

Bain, M.B., and Meixler, M.S., 2000, Defining a target fish community for planning and evaluating enhancement of the Quinebaug River in Massachusetts and Connecticut: Ithaca, NY, New York Cooperative Fish and Wildlife Research Unit, Cornell University, 20 p.

Bain, M.B., and Meixler, M.S., 2008, A target fish community to guide river restoration: River Research and Applications, v. 24, p. 453–458.

Baker, M.E., and King, R.S., 2010, A new method for detecting and interpreting biodiversity and ecological community thresholds: Methods in Ecology and Evolution, v. 1, no. 1, p. 25–37.

Bolker, B.M., 2008, Ecological models and data in R: Princeton, NJ, Princeton University Press, 396 p.

Brabec, Elizabeth, Schulte, Stacey, and Richards, P.L., 2002, Impervious surfaces and water quality—a review of current literature and its implications for watershed planning: Journal of Planning Literature, v. 16, no. 4, p. 499–514.

Brainwood, Meredith, Burgin, Shelley, and Byrne, Maria, 2008, The impact of small and large impoundments on freshwater mussel distribution in the Hawkesbury-Nepean River, Southeastern Australia: River Research and Applications, v. 24, p. 1325–1342.

Brown, L.R., Cuffney, T.F., Coles, J.E., Fitzpatrick, Faith, McMaahon, Gerard, Steuer, Jeffrey, Bell, A.H., and May, J.T., 2009a, Urban streams across the USA – lessons learned from studies in 9 metropolitan areas: Journal of the North American Benthological Society, v. 28, no. 4, p. 1051–1069.

Brown, L.R., Gregory, M.B., and May, J.T., 2009b, Relation of urbanization to stream fish assemblages and species traits in nine metropolitan areas of the United States: Urban Ecosystems, v. 12, p. 391–416.

Bunn, S.E., and Arthington, A.H., 2002, Basic principles and ecological consequences of altered flow regimes for aquatic biodiversity: Environmental Management, v. 30, no. 4, p. 492–507.

Burnham, K.P., and Anderson, D.R., 2002, Model selection and multimodel inference—a practical information-theoretic approach: New York, Springer-Verlag, 488 p.

Cade, B.S., and Guo, Q., 2000, Estimating effects of constraints on plant performance with regression quantiles: Oikos, v. 91, p. 245–254.

Cade, B.S., and Noon, B.R., 2003, A gentle introduction to quantile regression for ecologists: Frontiers in Ecology and the Environment, v. 1, no. 8, p. 412–420.

Cade, B.S., Noon, B.R., and Flather, C.H., 2005, Quantile regression reveals hidden bias and uncertainty in habitat models: Ecology, v. 83, no. 3, p. 786–800.

Cade, B.S., Terrell, J.T., and Schroeder, R.L., 1999, Estimating effects of limiting factors with regression quantiles: Ecology, v. 80, no. 1, p. 311–323

Carter, Timothy, Jackson, C.R., Rosemond, Amy, Pringle, Cathy, Raddcliffe, David, Tollner, William, Maez, John, Leigh, David, and Trice, Amy, 2009, Beyond the urban gradient—barriers and opportunities for timely studies of urbanization effects on aquatic ecosystems: Journal of the North American Benthological Society, v. 28, no. 4, p. 1038–1050.

Cereghino, R., Santoul, F., Compin, A., Figuerola, J., and Mastrorillo, S., 2005, Co-occurance patterns of some small bodied freshwater fishes in Southern France—Implications for fish conservation and environmental management: Ambio; v. 34, no. 6, p. 440–444.

Coles, J.F., Cuffney, T.F., McMahon, Gerard, and Beaulieu, K.M., 2004, The effects of urbanization on the biological, physical, and chemical characteristics of coastal New England streams: U.S. Geological Survey Professional Paper 1695, 47 p.

Coles, J.F., Cuffney, T.F., McMahon, Gerard, and Rosiu, C.J., 2010, Judging a brook by its cover—the relation between ecological condition of a stream and urban land cover in New England: Northeast Naturalist, v. 17, no. 1, p. 29–48.

Creque, S.M., Rutherford, E.S., and Zorn, T.G., 2005, Use of GIS-derived landscape-scale habitat features to explain spatial patterns of fish density in Michigan Rivers: North American Journal of Fisheries Management, v. 25, p. 1411–1425.

Cuffney, T.F., Brightbill, R.A., May, J.T., and Waite, I.A., in press, Responses of benthic macroinvertebrates to environmental changes associated with urbanization in nine metropolitan areas: Ecological Applications, accessed online on June 18, 2010, at *http://www.esajournals.org/doi/pdf/10.1890/08–1311.*

Cunningham, R.B., and Lindenmayer, D.B., 2005, Modeling count data of rare species: Some statistical issues: Ecology, v. 86, no. 5, p. 1135–1142.

Freeman, M.C., and Marcinek, P.A., 2006, Fish assemblage responses to water withdrawals and water supply reservoirs in Piedmont streams: Environmental Management, v. 38, no. 3, p. 435–450.

Gauch, H.G. Jr., 1982, Multivariate analysis in community ecology: New York, Cambridge University Press, 298 p.

Gawler, S.C., Anderson, M.G., Olivero, A.P., and Clark, Melissa, 2008, The Northeast habitat classification and mapping project—a report to the Virginia Department of Game and Inland Fisheries on behalf of the Northeast Association of Fish and Wildlife Agencies for the National Fish and Wildlife Foundation: NWFWF Project 2006-0181-003, accessed April 1, 2010, at *http://rcngrants.org/sites/default/files/NE_Hab_Class&Map_FinalRep_121608.pdf* .

Gido, K.B., Falke, J.A., Oakes, R.M., and Haze, K.J., 2006, Fish-habitat relations across spatial scales in prairie streams: American Fisheries Society Symposium, v. 48, p. 265–285.

Goldstein, R.M., and Meador, M.R., 2004, Comparison of fish species traits from small streams to large rivers: Transactions of the American Fisheries Society, v. 133, p. 971–983.

Halliwell, D.B., Langdon, R.W., Daniels, R.A., Kurtenbach, J.P., and Jacobson, R.A., 1999, Classification of freshwater fish species of the northeastern United States for use in the development of indices of biological integrity, with regional applications, *in* Simon, T.P., ed., Assessing the sustainability and biological integrity of water resources using fish communities: New York, CRC Press, p. 301–335.

Hartel, K.E., Halliwell, D.B., and Launer, A.E., 2002, Inland fishes of Massachusetts: Lincoln, MA, Massachusetts Audubon Society, 328 p.

Kanno, Y., and Vokoun, J.C., 2010, Evaluating effects of water withdrawals and impoundments on fish assemblages in southern New England streams, USA: Fisheries Management and Ecology, v. 17, no. 2, 12 p.

Karr, J.R., and Chu, E.W., 1999, Restoring life in running waters: Washington D.C., Island Press, 206 p.

Kashiwagi, Michael, and Richards, Todd, 2009, Development of target fish-community models for Massachusetts mainstem rivers: Boston, Commonwealth of Massachusetts Department of Fish and Game, Division of Fisheries and Wildlife Technical Report, 85 p.

Kennen, J.G., Riva-Murray, K., and Beaulieu, K.M., 2009, Determining hydrologic factors that influence stream macroinvertebrate assemblages in the northeastern US: Ecohydrology, v. 2, no. 1, p. 88–106.

King, R.S., and Baker, M.E., 2010, Considerations for analyzing ecological community thresholds in response to anthropogenic environmental gradients: Journal of the North American Benthological Society, v. 29, no. 3, p. 998–1008.

Koenker, R., 2005, Quantile regression: New York, Cambridge University Press, 349 p.

Koenker, R., and Machado, J.A.F., 1999, Goodness of fit and related inference processes for quantile regression: Journal of the American Statistical Association, v. 94, p. 1296–1310.

Konrad, C.P., Brasher, A.M.D., and May, J.T., 2008, Assessing streamflow characteristics as limiting factors on benthic invertebrate assemblages in streams across the western United States: Freshwater Biology, v. 53, no. 10, p. 1917–2131.

Legros, J.D., and Parasiewicz, Piotr, 2007, Development and analysis of a Target Fish-Community model to assess the biological integrity of the Lamprey Designated River, New Hampshire, and to identify indicator fish species for a MesoHABSIM model, accessed April 1, 2010, at *http://des.nh.gov/organization/divisions/water/wmb/ rivers/instream/lamprey/documents/tfc_report_ legros_21june2007final.pdf* .

Lewin, W., Freyhof, J., Volker, H., Mehner, T., Wolter, C., 2010, When no catches matter: Coping with zeros in environmental assessments: Ecological Indicators, v. 10, p. 572–583.

Mackey, P.C., Barlow, P.M., and Ries, K.G., III, 1998, Relations between discharge and wetted perimeter and other hydraulic-geometry characteristics at selected streamflow-gaging stations in Massachusetts: U.S. Geological Survey Water-Resources Investigations Report 98–4094, 44 p.

Martin, T.G., Wintle, B.A., Rhodes, J.R., Kuhnert, P.M., Low-Choy, S.J., Tyre, A.J., and Possingham, P., 2005, Zero tolerance ecology: improving ecological inference by modeling the source of zero observations: Ecological Letters , v. 8, p. 1235–1246.

Massachusetts Office of Geographic and Environmental Informations, 2007, Impervious surface datalayer for Massachusetts, accessed April 1, 2010, at *http://www.mass.gov/mgis/ impervious_surface.htm* .

McCullagh, P., and Nelder, J.A., 1989, Generalized Linear Models (2d ed.): London, Chapman and Hall, 532 p.

Meador, M.R., and Carlisle, D.M., 2009, Predictive models for fish assemblages in eastern U.S. streams—implications for assessing biodiversity: Transactions of the American Fisheries Society, v. 138, p. 725–740.

Meador, M.R., Carlisle, D.M., and Coles, J.F., 2008, Use of tolerance values to diagnose water-quality stressors to aquatic biota in New England streams: Ecological Indicators, v. 8, p. 718–728.

Meador, M.R., Coles, J.F., and Zappia, H., 2005, Fish assemblage responses to urban intensity gradients in contrasting metropolitan areas—Birmingham, Alabama, and Boston, Massachusetts, *in* Brown, L.R., Hughes R.M., Gray R., and Meador, M.R. , eds., Effects of urbanization on stream ecosystems: Bethesda, Md, American Fisheries Society AFS Symposium 47, p. 409–423.

Meixler, Marci, 2006, Defining a target fish community for the Charles River: Ithaca, NY, Cornell University Department of Natural Resources, 26 p., accessed April 1, 2010, at *http://environment.cornell.edu/people/mm/CRtargetfish.pdf* .

Olivero, A.P., and Anderson, M.G., 2008, Northeast aquatic habitat classification: Boston, The Nature Conservancy in collaboration with the Northeast Association of Fish and Wildlife Agencies, 45 p.

Parasiewicz, Piotr, 2004, Ecohydrology Study of the Quinebaug River—Final Report to the Project Management Committee and the New England Interstate Water Pollution Control Commission: Ithaca, NY, Cornell University Department of Natural Resources, Instream Habitat Program and the NY Cooperative Fish and Wildlife Research Unit, 385 p.

Parker, G.W., Armstrong, D.S., and Richards, T.A., 2004, Comparison of methods for determining streamflow requirements for aquatic habitat protection at selected sites on the Assabet and Charles Rivers, Eastern Massachusetts, 2000–2002: U.S. Geological Survey Scientific Investigations Report 2004–5092, 72 p.

Paul, M.J., and Meyer, J.L., 2001, Streams in the urban landscape: Annual Review of Ecology and Systematics, v. 32, p. 333–365.

Pearce, J., and Ferrier S., 2001, The practical value of modeling relative abundance of species for regional conservation planning: Biological Conservation, v. 98, p. 33–43.

Pickett, S.T.A., 1989, Space-for-time substitution as an alternative to long-term studies, *in* Likens, G.E., ed., Long-term studies in ecology–Approaches and alternatives: New York, Springer Verlag, p. 110–135.

Poff, N.L., Allen, J.D., Bain, M.B., Karr, J.R., Prestagaard, K.L., Richter, B.D., Sparks, R.E., and Stromberg, J.C., 1997, The natural flow regime–a paradigm for river conservation and restoration: Bioscience, v. 47, p. 769–784.

Poff, N.L., Richter, B.D., Arthington, A.H., Bunn, S.E., Naiman, R.J., Kendy, E., Acreman, M., Apse, C., Bledsoe, B.P., Freeman, M., Henriksen, J., Jacobson, R.B., Kennen, J., Merritt, D.M., O'Keeffe, J., Olden, J.D., Rogers, K., Tharme, R.E., and Warner, A., 2010, The Ecological Limits of Hydrologic Alteration (ELOHA)—a new framework for developing regional environmental flow standards: Freshwater Biology v. 55, p. 147–170.

Poff, N.L., and Zimmerman J.K.H., 2010, Ecological responses to altered flow regimes—a literature review to inform environmental flows science and management: Freshwater Biology, v. 55, p. 194–205.

Potts, J.M., and Elith, J., 2006, Comparing species abundance models: Ecological Modelling, v. 199, p. 153–163.

Price, A.L., and Peterson, J.T., 2010, Estimation and modeling of electrofishing capture efficiency for fishes in wadeable warmwater streams: North American Journal of Fisheries Management, v.30, , p. 481–498.

R Development Core Team, 2008, R—A language and environment for statistical computing: Vienna, Austria, R Foundation for Statistical Computing, ISBN 3-900051-07-0, accessed April 1, 2010, at *http://www.R-project.org* .

Randall, A.D., 2001, Hydrogeologic framework of stratified-drift aquifers in the glaciated northeastern United States: U.S. Geological Survey Professinal Paper 1415-B, 179 p.

Richter, B.D., Baumgartner, J.V., Wigington, Robert, and Braun, D.P., 1997, How much water does a river need?: Freshwater Biology, v. 37, p. 231–249.

Ries, K.G., III, 1997, August median streamflows in Massachusetts: U.S. Geological Survey Water-Resources Investigations Report 97–4190, 24 p.

Ries K.G., III, and Friesz, P.J., 2000, Methods for estimating low-flow statistics for Massachusetts streams: U.S. Geological Survey Water-Resources Investigations Report 99–4135, 81 p.

Roy, A.H., Freeman, M.C., Freeman, B.J., Wenger, S.J., Ensign, W.E., and Meyer, J.L., 2005, Investigating hydrologic alteration as a mechanism of fish assemblage shifts in urbanizing streams: Journal of the North American Benthological Society, v. 24, p. 656–678.

Roy, A.H., Purcell, A.H., Walsh, C.J., and Wenger, S.J., 2009, Urbanization and stream ecology—five years later: Journal of the North American Benthological Society, v. 28, no. 4, p. 908–910.

Scharf, F.S., Juanes, Francis, and Sutherland, Michael, 1998, Inferring ecological relationships from the edges of scatter diagrams—comparison of regression techniques: Ecology, v. 79, p. 448–460.

Schooley, R.L., and Wiens, J.A., 2005, Spatial ecology of cactus bugs: area constraints and patch connectivity: Ecology, v. 86, p. 1627–1639.

Sileshi, G., Hailu, G., and Nyadzi, G., 2009, Traditional occupancy-abundance models are inadequate for zero-inflated ecological count data: Ecological Modelling, v. 220, p. 1764–1775.

Snelder, T.N., and Lamouroux, Nicolas, 2010, Co-variation of fish assemblages, flow regimes and other habitat factors in French rivers: Freshwater Biology, v. 55, p. 881–892.

Thomson, J.D., Weiblen, G., Thomson, B.A., Alfaro, S., and Legendre, P., 1996, Untangling multiple factors in spatial distributions—lilies, gophers, and rocks: Ecology, v. 77, p. 1698–1715.

Trebitz, A.S., Brazner, J.C., Danz, N.P., Pearson, M.S., Peterson, G.S., Tanner, D.K., Taylor, D.L., West, C.W., and Hollenhorst, T.P., 2009, Geographic, anthropogenic, and habitat influences on Great Lakes coastal wetland fish assemblages: Canadian Journal of Fisheries and Aquatic Sciences, v. 66, p. 1328–1342.

University of New Hampshire, University of Massachusetts, and Normandeau Associates, Inc., 2008, Development and Analysis of Target Fish-Community Models to Evaluate the Status of the Existing Fish Communities in the Upper and Lower Souhegan River, Appendix 6, *in* Souhegan River Protected Instream Flow Report: Concord, NH, New Hampshire Department Of Environmental Services, NHDES-R-WD-06-50, accessed April 1, 2010, at *http://des. nh.gov/organization/divisions/water/wmb/rivers/instream/ souhegan/study.htm.*

U. S. Geological Survey, 1999a, The national elevation dataset, accessed July 23, 1999, at *http://edcnts12.cr.usgs. gov/ned/factsheet. asp.*

U.S. Geological Survey, 1999b, The national hydrography dataset: U.S. Geological Survey Fact Sheet 106-99, accessed April 2000 to March 2001 at *http://nhd.usgs.gov/.*

U.S. Geological Survey, 2000, National land-cover data (NLCD) circa 1992: completed nationwide September 2000, accessed October 27, 2003, at *http://seamless.usgs. gov/.*

VanSickle, John, Baker, Joan, Herlily, Alan, Bayley, Peter, Gregory, Stanley, Haggerty, Patti, Ashkenas, Linda, and Li, Judith, 2004, Projecting the biological condition of streams under alternative scenarios of human land use: Ecological applications, v. 14, no. 2, p. 368–380.

VanSickle, John, and Johnson, C.B., 2008, Parametric distance weighting of landscape influence on streams: Landscape Ecology, v. 23, p. 427–438.

Vaz, Sandrine, Martine, C.S., Eastwood, P.D., Ernande, Bruno, Carpentier, Andre, Meaden, G.J., and Coppin, Frank, 2008, Modelling species distributions using regression quantiles: Journal of Applied Ecology, v. 45, p. 204–217.

Vuong, Q.H., 1989, Likelihood ratio tests for model selection and non-nested hypotheses: Econometrica, v. 57, no. 2, p. 307–333.

Walsh, C.J., Roy, A.H., Feminella, J.W., Cottingham, P.D., Groffman, P.M., and Morgan, R.P.II, 2005, The urban stream sundrome—a current knowledge and the search for a cure: Journal of the North American Benthological Society, v. 25, no. 3, p. 706–723.

Wang, Lizhu, Brenden, Travis, Seelbach, Paul, Cooper, Arthur, Allan, David, Clark, Richard Jr., and Wiley, Michael, 2008, Landscape based identification of human disturbance gradients and reference conditions for Michigan streams: Environmental Monitoring and Assessment, v. 14, no. 1, p. 1–17.

Wang, Lizhu, Infante, Dana, Lyons, John, Stewart, Jana, and Cooper, Arthur, 2010, Effects of dams in river networks on fish assemblages in non-impounded sections of rivers in Michigan and Wisconsin: River Research and Applications, accessed June 1, 2010, at *http://dx.doi.org/10.1002/rra.1356*.

Wang, Lizhu, Lyons, John, and Kanehl, Paul, 2001a, Impacts of urbanization on stream habitat and fish across multiple spatial scales: Environmental Management, v. 28, no. 2, p. 255–266.

Wang, Lizhu, Lyons, John, and Kanehl, Paul, 2001b, Impacts of urban land cover on trout streams in Wisconsin and Minnesota: Transactions of the American Fisheries Society, v. 132, p. 825–839.

Weiskel, P.K., Brandt, S.L., DeSimone, L.A., Ostiguy, L.J., and Archfield, S.A., 2010, Indicators of streamflow alteration, habitat fragmentation, impervious cover, and water quality for Massachusetts stream basins: U.S. Geological Survey Scientific Investigations Report 2009–5272, 79 p.

Weiskel, P.K., Vogel, R.M., Steeves, P.A., Zarriello, P.J., DeSimone, L.A., and Ries, K.G., 2007, Water use regimes – characterizing direct human interactions with hydrologic systems: Water Resources Research, v. 43, 11 p.

Wenger, S.J., and Freeman, M.C., 2008, Estimating species occurrence, abundance, and detection probability using zero-inflated distributions: Ecology, v. 89, no. 10, p. 2953–2959.

Wenger, S.J., Peterson, J.T., Freeman, M.C., Freeman, B.J., and Homans, D.D., 2008, Stream fish occurrence in response to impervious cover, historic land use, and hydrogeomorphic factors: Canadian Journal of Fisheries and Aquatic Sciences, v. 65, pp. 1250–1264.

Wenger, S.J., Roy, A.H., Jackson, C.R., Bernhardt, E.S., Carter, T.L., Filoso, Solange, Gibson, C.A., Hession, W.C., Kaushal, S.S., Marti, Euginia, Meyer, J.L., Palmer, M.A., Paul, M.J., Purcell, A.H., Ramirex, Alonso, Rosemond, A.D., Schofield, K.A., Sudduth, E.B., and Walsh, C.A., 2009, Twenty-six key research questions in urban stream ecology—an assessment of the state of the science: Journal of the North American Benthological Society, v. 28, no. 4, p. 1080–1098.

Whitworth, W.R., 1996, Freshwater fishes of Connecticut: Connecticut Department of Environmental Protection Bulletin 114, 243 p.

Wickham, J.D., Wu, Jianguo, and Bradford, D.F., 1997, A conceptual framework for selecting and analyzing stressor data to study species richness at large spatial scales: Environmental Management, v. 21, no. 2, p. 247–257.

Wilding, T.K., and Poff, N.L., 2008, Flow ecology relationships for the watershed flow evaluation tool, accessed April 1, 2010, at *http://cwcb.state.co.us/NR/rdonlyres/3ECA858C-9305-4EA7-ACF8-7EE8FA41646E/0/WFETAppB.pdf*.

Zarriello, P.J., Parker, G.W., Armstrong, A.S., and Carlson, C.S., in press, Effects of water use and land use on streamflow and aquatic habitat in the Sudbury and Assabet River Basins, Massachusetts; Chapter 1– Simulated effects of water use, and projected water-use and land-use change on streamflow with a precipitation-runoff model; Chapter 2– Fish communities, stream temperature, and assessment of minimum streamflow targets for aquatic habitat at selected sites: U.S. Geological Survey Scientific Investigations Report 2010–5042.

Zeileis, A., Kleiber, C., and Jackman, S., 2008, Regression models for count data in R: Journal of Statistical Software, v. 27, no. 8, accessed April 1, 2010, at *http://www.jstatsoft.org/v27/i08/*.

Zheng, B., and Agresti, A., 2000, Summarizing the predictive power of a generalized linear model: Statistics in Medicine, v. 19, p. 1771–1781.

Zorn, T.G., Seelbach, P.W., Rutherford, E.S., Wills, T.C., Cheng, S.-T., and Wiley, M.J., 2008, A regional-scale habitat suitability model to assess the effects of flow reduction on fish assemblages in Michigan streams: Ann Arbor, MI, Michigan Department of Natural Resources, Fisheries Research Report 2089, 46 p.

Zorn, T.G., Seelbach, P.W., and Wiley, M.J., 2004, Utility of species specific, multiple linear regression models for prediction of fish assemblages in rivers of Michigan's lower peninsula: Lansing, MI, State of Michigan Department of Natural Resources, Fisheries Division, Fisheries Research Report 2072, 51 p.

Zorn, T.G., Seelbach, P.W., and Wiley, M.J., 2009, Relations between habitat and fish density in Michigan streams: Lansing, MI, State of Michigan Department of Natural Resources, Fisheries Division, Fisheries Research Report 2091, 60 p.

Zuur, A.F., Ieno, E.N., Walker, N.J., Saveliev, A.A., and Smith, G.M., 2009, Mixed effects models and extensions in ecology with R: New York, Springer Science + Business Media, LLC, 574 p.

Zuur, A.F., Ieno, E.N., Smith, G.M., 2007, Analyzing ecological data: New York, Springer Science + Business Media, LLC, 672 p.

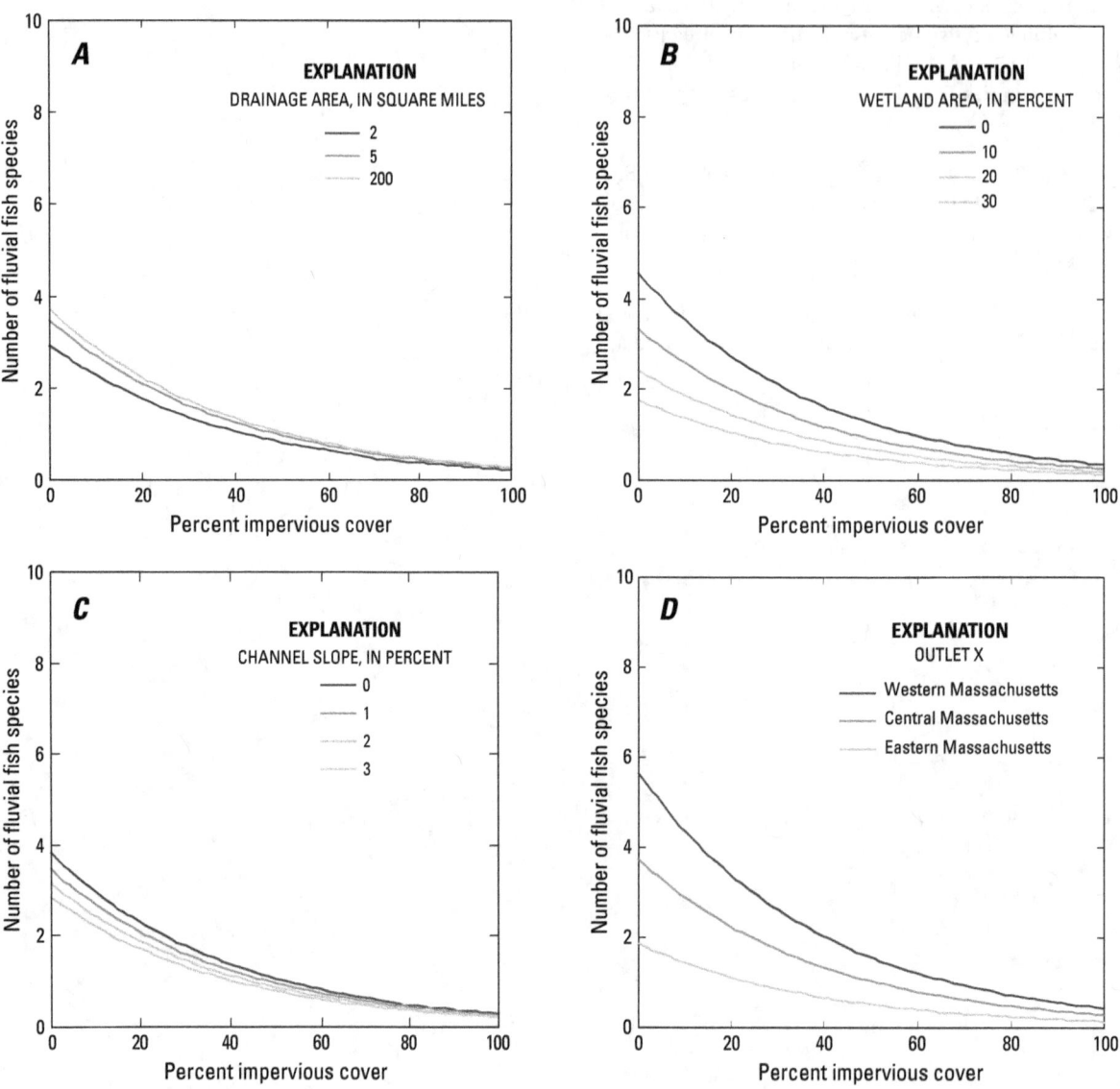

Figure 20.   Generalized linear model output for relations among fluvial-fish species richness, percent impervious cover, and (*A*) drainage area, (*B*) wetland area, (*C*) channel slope, and (*D*) outlet X for selected Massachusetts streams, 1998–2008.

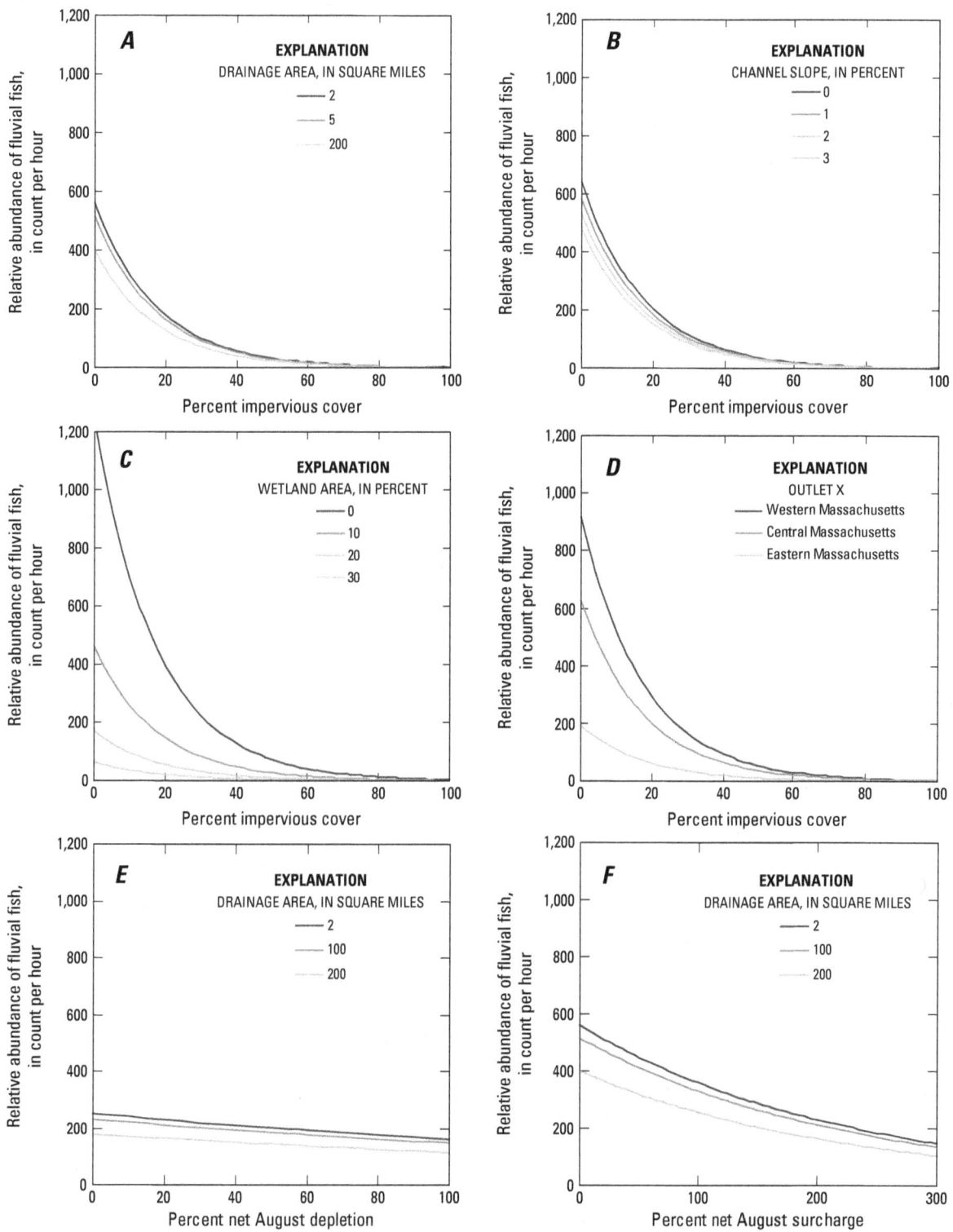

Figure 21. Generalized linear model output for relations among relative abundance of fluvial fish, percent impervious cover, or percent net August depletion or surcharge, and (*A*) drainage area, (*B*) channel slope, (*C*) wetland area, (*D*) outlet X, (*E*) drainage area, (*F*) drainage area, (*G*) channel slope, (*H*) channel slope, (*I*) wetland area, (*J*) wetland area, (*K*) outlet X, and (*L*) outlet X for selectd Massachusetts streams, 1998–2008.

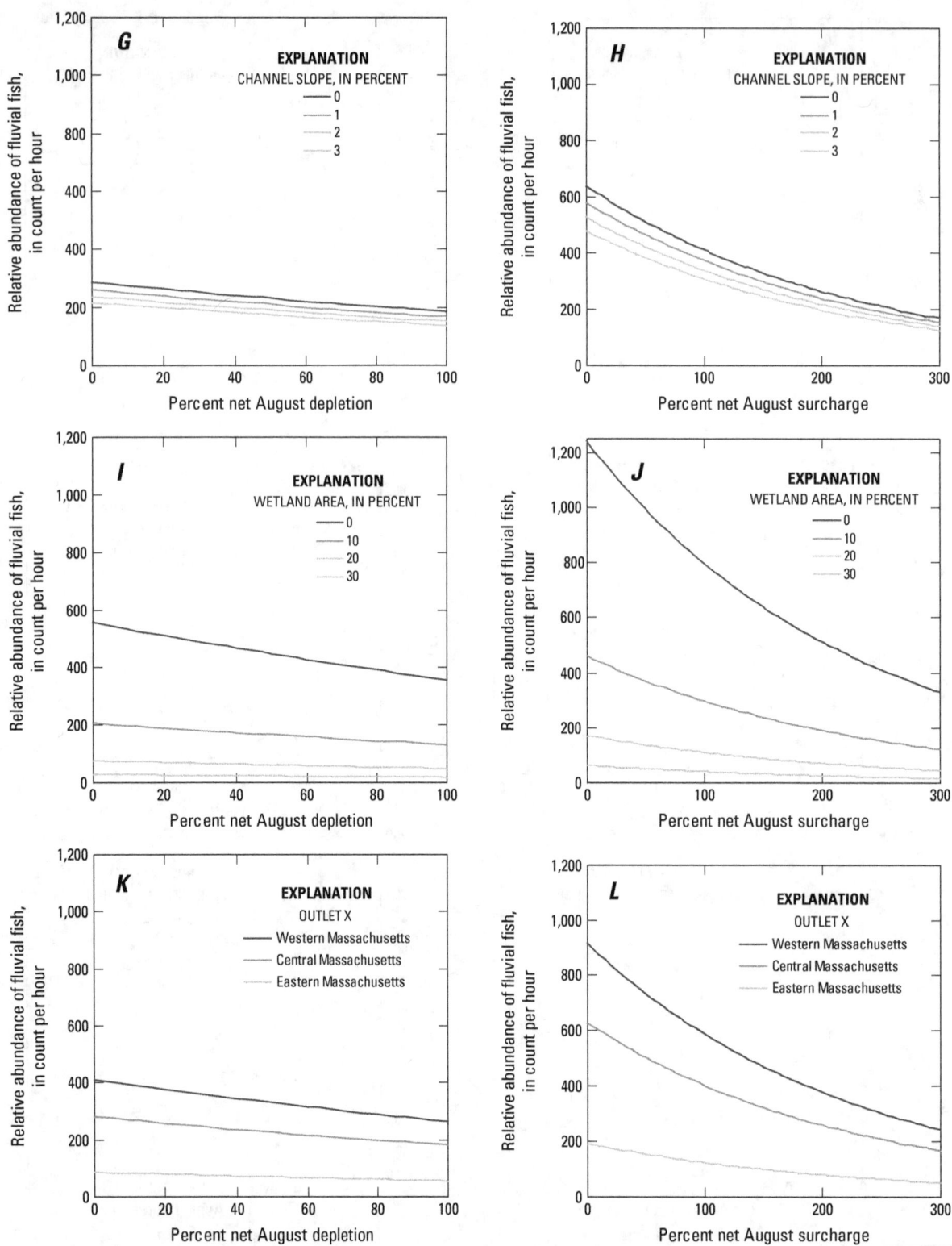

Figure 21.   Generalized linear model output for relations among relative abundance of fluvial fish, percent impervious cover, or percent net August depletion or surcharge, and (*A*) drainage area, (*B*) channel slope, (*C*) wetland area, (*D*) outlet X, (*E*) drainage area, (*F*) drainage area, (*G*) channel slope, (*H*) channel slope, (*I*) wetland area, (*J*) wetland area, (*K*) outlet X, and (*L*) outlet X for selected Massachusetts streams, 1998–2008.—Continued.

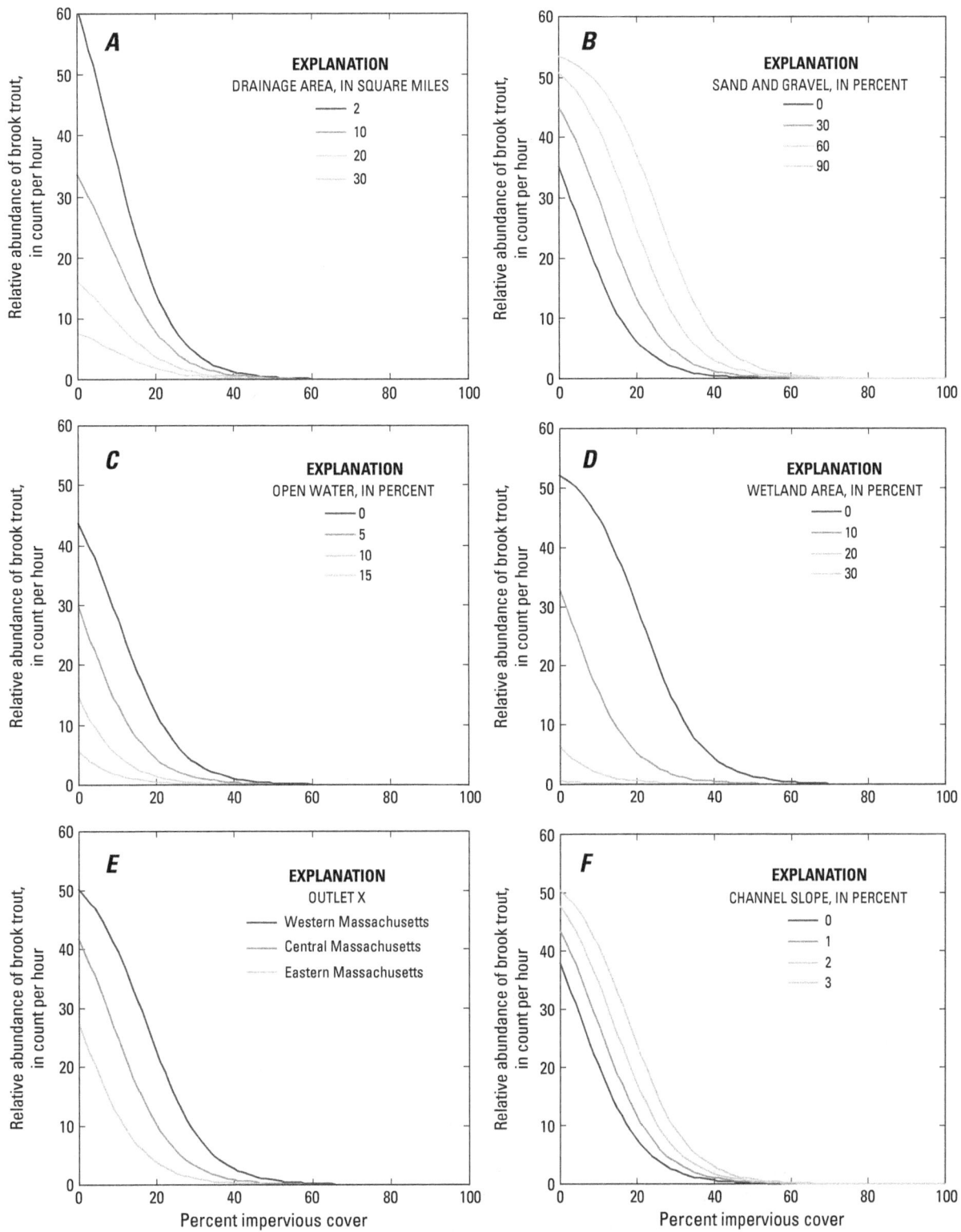

Figure 22. Generalized linear model output for relations among relative abundance of brook trout, percent impervious cover, and (*A*) drainage area, (*B*) sand and gravel, (*C*) open water, (*D*) wetland area, (*E*) outlet X, and (*F*) channel slope for selected Massachusetts streams, 1998–2008.

Prepared by the West Trenton Publishing Service
Center. For more information concerning the
research in this report, contact:
Director
USGS Massachusetts-Rhode Island
Water Science Center 10 Bearfoot Road Northborough,
MA 01532

or visit our Web site at:
http://ma.water.usgs.gov